Rail freight since

...NERS,
AND
...CIAL
TRAFFICS

Rail freight since 1968

CONTAINERS, CARS AND SPECIAL TRAFFICS

Paul Shannon

· RAILWAY HERITAGE ·
from
The NOSTALGIA Collection

First published in 2010

British Library Cataloguing in Publication Data

A catalogue record for this book is available from the British Library.

ISBN 978 1 85794 347 4

Silver Link Publishing Ltd
The Trundle
Ringstead Road
Great Addington
Kettering
Northants NN14 4BW

Tel/Fax: 01536 330588
email: sales@nostalgiacollection.com
Website: www.nostalgiacollection.com

Printed and bound in the Czech Republic

All photographs are by the author unless otherwise credited.

Half title The single-track branch from Skelton Junction to Partington saw intermittent use in the late 1980s for block trains of propylene from Baglan Bay to the Shell plant at Partington. No 47322 has just run round train 6V71, the 1658 propylene empties from Partington to Baglan Bay, at Skelton Junction on 25 March 1989. The train would continue its journey via Altrincham, Middlewich and Crewe.

Opposite title page At Southampton, deep-sea container traffic quickly outgrew the capacity of Millbrook and Freightliner opened the more conveniently situated Maritime terminal on the south side of the line. No 47002 prepares to uncouple from its train at Southampton Maritime after arriving with 4O71, the 1350 service from Willesden, on 18 August 1987.

Below Washwood Heath yard was the main gathering point for West Midlands automotive traffic from the 1970s until 2008. The yard was remodelled in the 1990s in connection with the building of the A47 road, which now skirts the northern edge of the yard; it also gained high-security fencing for Channel Tunnel traffic. On 27 May 1998 No 47284 leaves Washwood Heath with 6G52, the 0804 trip working to Bordesley. On the right is a trainload of Citroën and Peugeot cars waiting to be delivered to the GEFCO depot at Corby.

Contents

Preface

This final volume in the 'Rail freight since 1968' series deals with a diverse range of rail freight types, all of which fall outside the 'bulk freight' category but which have tended to move in full trainloads rather than by the wagonload.

Intermodal traffic was relatively new to the railway in the late 1960s, with the Freightliner network still in its infancy but developing fast. Dr Beeching saw containers as the replacement for domestic wagonload traffic, offering the efficiencies of trainload operation while providing many different customers with a door-to-door service. For a time that idea seemed to succeed, but the costs of road-rail transfer at both ends of the journey became prohibitive for many flows, and even on very long hauls, such as London to Aberdeen, Freightliner struggled to make a profit. What saved Freightliner, and indeed helped it to thrive from the 1980s onwards, was the rapid growth of deep-sea containers, where high volumes could be concentrated on a small number of trunk routes and where transhipment was required at the port regardless of whether the onward journey was by rail or road. Even then, the railway has had to work hard to keep up with the ever larger size of deep-sea containers, necessitating expensive route upgrades as well as the use of special low-deck wagons. The Channel Tunnel was meant to herald a new dawn for UK intermodal traffic, but ended up being nothing short of an embarrassing disappointment. As for the domestic market, innovative bi-modal systems such as 'Piggyback' and 'Roadrailer' failed to become established, but conventional containers and swapbodies managed to compete effectively on a few long-distance routes, notably between Daventry and the Central Belt of Scotland.

Cars and car parts were another growth area for rail freight from the 1960s onwards – a case of the railway making some gain, albeit small, from its biggest competitor. Both Ford and the variously named group of companies that ended up as Rover geared some of their primary distribution to rail haulage. As the UK car industry shrank in favour of imports, so the railway adapted by running trains from ports such as Sheerness and Portbury. The economics of distributing cars by rail were sometimes difficult and even the long-haul traffic via the Channel Tunnel did not grow as the railway had hoped.

Freightliner entered the automotive market but had to withdraw because it could not make it pay. As with many freight flows, the prospects for the automotive business are best where trains can run loaded in both directions, as happened for many years between Garston and Dagenham.

Chemicals, irradiated nuclear fuel and milk are a diverse set of traffics for which the railway developed special wagons and, in many cases, special train services. The movement of irradiated nuclear fuel is more or less captive to rail and provided the basis for one of the more successful open access freight operations, Direct Rail Services, in the 1990s. The flows of chemicals and milk were anything but captive, with very little chemicals traffic remaining on rail by the 21st century and milk having failed to make a comeback after its demise in the early 1980s.

Finally, this volumes deals with parcels, mail and newspaper traffic – an area of railway operation that often gets overlooked as it falls between the passenger and freight spheres. Although the loss of Travelling Post Office trains and the collapse of the Royal Mail contract in 2003 were well publicised, the longer-term decline in 'van trains' happened gradually, and individual losses were not well documented. Parcels traffic had much in common with wagonload freight, in that the railway aimed to provide a nationwide service by combining lots of small consignments into larger units for trunk haulage. The costs of transferring packages between rail and road and of running a complex network of interconnecting trains became prohibitive and the only operation to survive in 2010 was the slick, high-volume flow of mail between three depots on the West Coast Main Line.

The previous volumes in the Rail Freight since 1968 series:

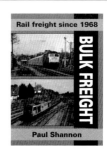

1.

Intermodal

The origins of railborne container traffic go back to the 1930s, when the railway companies introduced small containers that could be carried on two-axle flat wagons and transhipped between rail and road at any station goods yard equipped with a suitable crane. The objective was to address ever-increasing road competition by providing a door-to-door service for small consignments of goods without incurring the time and expense of loading and unloading the contents of wagons. BR developed the concept and introduced more than 20,000 two-axle 'Conflat' wagons in the 1950s to carry various types of container. Some of the containers were designed for special traffics such as frozen foods or bulk minerals, but most were standard boxes suitable for loads such as furniture and consumer goods.

Unfortunately the maximum loading for a standard 'B'-type container was just 4 tons and most of the traffic was subject to the inefficiencies of the BR wagonload network. Among the few examples of trainload container traffic was the 75mph 'Condor' service between Hendon and Gushetfaulds, which became well known because of its Metrovick Co-Bo haulage, but fell victim to road competition in 1965 after just six years of operation. BR attempted to revitalise the business by introducing lighter-weight 'Speedfreight' containers, capable of taking a 10-ton payload. But the technology was fundamentally obsolete and the use of 'Conflat' wagons for general merchandise traffic ceased in the mid-1970s, leaving just one or two specialised flows – such as dolofrit from Whitwell to Ravenscraig, which was carried in 4-ton 'L'-type containers mounted on 'Conflat L' wagons – to linger to the end of the decade.

Container traffic as we recognise it today was spearheaded by the Freightliner revolution of the mid-1960s. Undaunted by abortive trials with the USA-inspired 'Roadrailer', which conveyed specially adapted road trailers, BR decided in 1963 to develop a system for transporting International Standards Organisation (ISO) containers between purpose-built terminals at passenger train speeds. The Beeching Report recommended the setting up of a national network of liner trains as the most promising strategy for retaining non-bulk freight on rail. The advantages of such a network were summarised in the Report as follows:

(i)   Fast through working of trains to cheapen the trunk haul
(ii)   Containers designed for easy loading by forklift trucks through full-width end and side doors
(iii)   Elimination of the expensive double handling associated with the transfer of non-containerised freight from road to rail, and vice versa
(iv)   Elimination of expensive wagon movement on rail to assemble freight from small terminals into trains
(v)   Elimination of marshalling and absence of all shunting shocks
(vi)   Fast, reliable, scheduled delivery
(vii)   Freedom from pilferage
(viii)   Drastic reduction of documentation
(ix)   A system that is simple and readily understandable
(x)   Door-to-door costs below road costs for distances of about 100 miles and very substantially below for longer hauls

The Report envisaged a network that would serve more than 40 regional terminals and would carry some 57 million tons of freight per annum by 1984. The traffic projections for individual routes ranged from more than 2 million tonnes between Liverpool and London to just 10,000 tonnes on services such as Stockton to Grimsby and Reading to Bristol.

A set of four prototype liner train wagons was outshopped from Shildon Works early in 1964. Their design was innovative in a number of respects: the four wagons were semi-permanently connected by bar couplings, they had a skeletal framework instead of a solid floor, each wagon had a usable length of 42ft 6in, and they were among the first British wagons to be equipped with air instead of vacuum brakes. The brand name Freightliner was quickly adopted and follow-up wagon orders were placed with Ashford Works, enabling the first revenue-earning Freightliner train to run from Maiden Lane (north London) to Glasgow Gushetfaulds on 15 November 1965. The National Union of Railwaymen had delayed the launch because it had objected to private road hauliers being allowed access to Freightliner terminals and had also demanded the provision of guard's cabooses rather than allowing the guard to travel in the rear cab of the locomotive. On both counts the union eventually had to concede.

By March 1968 BR was serving 17 Freightliner terminals, as listed in the accompanying table. The absence of maritime terminals from the list is notable; even Southampton Millbrook, which later specialised in deep-sea boxes, was originally designed for domestic traffic. Additionally, some Freightliner trains served non-Freightliner terminals, such as Camden Goods, which had a daily service to and from Heysham Port. Anglo-Scottish Freightliner links included a daily train between Thames Wharf and Govan and the 'Tartan Arrow' service between Kentish Town and Glasgow Bridgeton. During 1968 BR introduced a Freightliner service between Park Royal (West London) and Par, calling at Plymouth en route; however, this service only lasted until 1970. Another short-lived service operated from 1968 until 1970 between Stratford and Paris, with the wagons crossing the Channel on the Dover to Dunkerque train ferry.

Freightliner terminals, March 1968	
Aberdeen	Garston
Glasgow Gushetfaulds	Dudley
Edinburgh	Willesden
Newcastle	York Way (north London)
Stockton	King's Cross
Leeds	Stratford
Hull	Cardiff Pengam
Sheffield	Southampton Millbrook
Longsight	

Under the 1968 Transport Act Freightliner Ltd was established as a separate company from BR, operating as part of the National Freight Corporation. Freightliner Ltd took ownership of BR's ISO containers, but leased the wagons and terminals from BR, which also continued to provide diesel and electric traction. The network of container trains continued to grow, with 49 routes in operation by 1969. New regional terminals were opened at Nottingham, Swansea, Trafford Park and Birmingham Landor Street, the last two supplementing the existing facilities at Longsight and Dudley respectively. Freightliner wagons were also used on some company trains, such as between Halewood and Harwich for the Ford Motor Company and, from 1970, between Linwood and Gosford Green (Coventry) for the Rootes group.

The Freightliner wagon fleet in December 1969 consisted of approximately 1,500 vehicles. All were built to a common design, similar to the prototype wagons introduced in 1964 but with a longer usable platform of 62ft 6in. Most were built at British Rail Engineering Limited's Ashford Works, but some were produced at Shildon. The wagons were designed to operate in permanently coupled sets of five, with only the two outer wagons having conventional buffing gear. Once the TOPS computer system came on stream, the outer wagons would be coded FGA and the inner wagons FFA. Each wagon could carry up to two 30-foot or three 20-foot containers; they could also take 10-foot containers, but these soon became obsolete as shippers opted for larger loads.

The early 1970s signalled a major change of direction for Freightliner, as it entered the market for distributing deep-sea ISO containers between ports and inland terminals. The extent of this shift had not been envisaged by Beeching, but it was to ensure the survival of Freightliner's intermodal division into the 21st century, with purely domestic container movements showing a steady decline in the face of road competition.

The port of Tilbury gained its Freightliner terminal in 1970, with services to Leeds, Birmingham and Manchester (Barton Dock). The first rail container terminal at Felixstowe, later to be known as Felixstowe South, opened in 1972. That same year brought the opening of Southampton Maritime Container Terminal, relieving the pressure on the original Millbrook site as the increase in deep-sea traffic gathered pace. Two rail-served facilities were established at the port of Ipswich, one at Cliff Quay on the east side of the Orwell estuary and the other at Griffin Wharf on the west side. Among the flows handled at Griffin Wharf was steel coil from South Wales. Ipswich yard became a busy hub for Freightliner

Framed by one of Aberdeen's fine semaphore signal gantries, No 47072 sets out with a Glasgow-bound Freightliner train on 2 September 1977. *Gavin Morrison*

services to and from Felixstowe and the two Ipswich terminals.

Freightliner's inland terminals became increasingly geared to maritime traffic during the 1970s. A new terminal at Barking Ripple Lane was opened in 1972 for specific trainload flows, including two daily services to and from Southampton for shipping lines OCL and ACT. A mini-terminal was established at Swindon to receive trainloads of Anchor butter from Tilbury. Overall, the proportion of deep-sea containers on Freightliner services rose from 13% in 1970 to 42% in 1980.

Freightliner also worked hard to develop its Irish traffic via Holyhead, which had been temporarily diverted to a makeshift terminal at Caernarfon between 1970 and 1972 because of the Menai Bridge fire. The Irish business included two types of 'land bridge' traffic: deep-sea containers routed via Birmingham, and European traffic to and from Harwich. Freightliner operated its own terminals in both Belfast and Dublin, and for a time the Irish rail operator CIE provided a connecting rail service from the quayside in Dublin.

Notable domestic successes for Freightliner in the 1970s included aluminium traffic from Rogerstone in South Wales and substantial Post Office business. On the debit side, Freightliner

Leeds Freightliner terminal

Opened in July 1967 on the site of Stourton steam shed, Leeds Freightliner terminal remained one of the UK's busiest inland distribution points for railborne containers in the early years of the 21st century. It lived through several changes in ownership and thrived on the shift in Freightliner business from domestic to deep-sea traffic.

Physically, the terminal occupies an 11-acre site on the south side of the former Midland Railway main line between Leeds and Normanton. Rail loading and unloading takes place on three double-ended sidings, all spanned by two overhead gantry cranes. The sidings can take 24-wagon trains, which is longer than at Freightliner's other inland terminals and a useful feature in reducing the amount of shunting when full-length trains arrive and depart. There are also two through Network Rail sidings between the terminal and the main line – known as the Arrival and Departure Line and Stourton Down Siding – which are available for stabling Freightliner trains when the terminal lines are full. Further wagon stabling is possible on the siding that once gave access to a steel terminal on the south side of the Freightliner compound.

One of the gantry cranes is a Morris 0-4-0 type (ie spanning 4 track widths between its legs and 0 track widths on each side), dating back to the opening of the terminal in 1967 but since modernised with an electronic grapple frame and new bogies. The other gantry crane is an Aumund 0-4-1 design, installed at Leeds in the 1990s. Together these gantry cranes take the lion's share of box movements to and from trains. Other lifting equipment at the terminal includes three reach stackers and two empty container handlers.

The total number of containers passing through the terminal each day is typically between 350 and 400. An increasing share of the business is carried in 9ft 6in 'high cube' containers, requiring the use of low-deck or 'pocket' wagons on routes from Southampton and Thamesport that have not yet benefited from loading gauge enhancement. Road collection and delivery is provided both by Freightliner and by independent hauliers, with destinations spread throughout Yorkshire and sometimes beyond. There is a considerable overlap between the areas served by Leeds and by neighbouring Freightliner terminals such as Wilton and Trafford Park.

An essential feature of ISO deep-sea containers is that they are stackable, which enables good use to be made of storage space. An imposing stack of deep-sea boxes overlooks Leeds Freightliner terminal on 19 February 2004, as No 66536 waits to depart with train 4L85, the 0858 to Ipswich.

No 66572 waits on the main line beside Leeds Freightliner terminal with train 4E01, the 0214 from Southampton Maritime, on the same day. Once the terminal is ready, the train will run forward a short distance and set back into the unloading sidings.

The compact nature of Leeds Freightliner terminal means that container storage space is at a premium. However, there is capacity for 200 TEU (Twenty-foot Equivalent Units) laden and 1,500 TEU unladen, which is greater than at any other inland Freightliner site. Although International Standards Organisation (ISO) containers are designed to be stacked up to 12 high, in practice Leeds Freightliner stack them to a maximum height of four. This allows them to be handled efficiently and also reduces the risk of a disaster in high winds. A grant from the Strategic Rail Authority in 2002 helped to fund new storage facilities and upgraded road access.

The train plan for Leeds in early 2010 comprised six daily arrivals from and departures to key deep-sea ports: two from/to Southampton, two from/to Felixstowe, and one each to/from Tilbury and Thamesport.

Until 2002 traffic could also be conveyed between Leeds and other inland terminals via the Freightliner hub at Crewe, but Freightliner decided to operate direct services rather than a 'hub and spoke' system to increase service reliability. In 2006 Freightliner withdrew the feeder service between Wilton and Leeds, which used to form part of a Leeds to Southampton train.

The move towards full trainload working allowed Freightliner to withdraw the pilot locomotive that shunted at Leeds until 2002. The only regular shunting tasks carried out today – all using main-line traction – are moving fully laden departures from the terminal sidings to Stourton Down Siding in order to vacate terminal space for the next arrival, and transferring 'pocket' wagons between different services to cater for 9ft 6in boxes to and from Southampton and Thamesport as required. Most shunt movements at the terminal require access to Network Rail infrastructure, now under the control of York since the closure of Stourton signal box in July 2002.

Left The former Great North of Scotland Railway goods yard at Elgin was equipped with a gantry crane to handle BR containers. No 25230 heads a short container train during loading at Elgin on 25 September 1980. Just behind the locomotive is a whisky tank, which operated between Dalmuir and the Chivas distillery at Keith. The use of Elgin as an intermodal railhead continued intermittently into the 1990s and even into the early years of the 21st century, although there was never enough traffic to sustain a regular service.

Above Carrying almost exclusively Freightliner's own branded containers, a northbound train comprising two five-vehicle FFA/FGA wagon sets approaches Watford Junction behind No 81004 on 16 April 1981.

Left Freightliner traffic was a rarity on the Woodhead route. Nos 76021 and 76026 pass Torside with a westbound Freightliner train on 16 June 1981, just five weeks before the closure of the line.

Above **Beer kegs, chemicals and aluminium products provide the load for 4M55, the 1825 Freightliner train from Newcastle to Trafford Park, as it crosses Durham Viaduct on 18 May 1982. The traction is No 45077.**

Right **Ipswich yard still contained a good mixture of freight traffic on 8 April 1983, as Nos 37105 and 37001 shunt a rake of Freightliner vehicles and VDA vans, ready to form a trip working to Felixstowe.**

Once electrification was extended to Ipswich, the yard would become the traction change point for many Freightliner trains to and from Felixstowe.

RLeft **Felixstowe was one of Freightliner's fastest growing traffic centres in the 1980s, as deep-sea traffic came to dominate the Freightliner network. The same pair of Class 37s as in the previous picture approach Felixstowe Beach level crossing with 4S80, the 1910 departure to Coatbridge, also on 8 April 1983.**

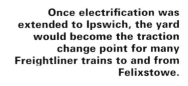

Above No 40086 passes Helsby station's co-acting semaphores with 4H59, the 0525 Holyhead to Trafford Park Freightliner train, on 6 July 1983. At that time Holyhead had four daily Freightliner departures, serving Crewe, Trafford Park, Birmingham and Stratford.

Below Newhaven never gained a permanent Freightliner terminal, but the port did handle Freightliner traffic as required. No 33060 pulls a uniform load of ISO containers out on to the main line at Newhaven Town on 26 August 1983.

Pairs of Class 37s were once the norm on many Freightliner trains from Tilbury and the East Anglian ports. Nos 37060 and 37116 pass the Procter & Gamble terminal at West Thurrock with 4M74, the 1358 Tilbury to Garston service, on 18 April 1984.

Freightliner trains from Trafford Park to Holyhead followed a circuitous route via the Fallowfield loop, Ashburys and Manchester Victoria in order to join the Chat Moss line to Earlestown. No 47142 passes Ordsall Lane Junction with 4D59, the 1554 departure from Trafford Park, on 26 April 1984.

Daytime Freightliner trains across the Pennines have never been particularly common, largely because rail struggles to compete with road on short journeys such as Immingham to Manchester and Liverpool to Leeds. A visit to Marsden on 10 November 1984 finds No 56131 about to enter Standedge Tunnel with a 4Z88 special working to Trafford Park.

closed its Sheffield terminal because of dwindling traffic volumes – largely the result of the declining stainless steel industry, coupled with improvements to the motorway network in South Yorkshire.

Further investment in deep-sea Freightliner traffic included the opening in 1978 of the Northfleet Hope terminal at Tilbury, operated by Tilbury Container Services and reached by a spur from Freightliner's own Tilbury terminal. In the same year the Department of Transport made a £412,000 Section 8 Grant towards the cost of a rail container terminal at

Right **The fourth departure of the day from Holyhead Freightliner terminal was a feeder service to Crewe Basford Hall, where the wagons would join a trunk train to Southampton. No 47106 departs from Holyhead with 4K59, the 1705 train to Crewe, on 17 April 1985.**

Below **The Tottenham & Hampstead line via Gospel Oak provided a convenient route for trains between Tilbury and the West Coast main line, avoiding the busy stretch of Great Eastern main line between Forest Gate and Stratford. Nos 37168 and 37052 pass Junction Road Junction, just east of Gospel Oak, with train 4M74 from Tilbury to Garston on 6 August 1985.**

16

Seaforth Dock, Liverpool. This project included 2 miles of new track and gave a welcome boost to rail freight in Liverpool at a time when conventional wagon traffic to and from the port had ceased completely. Freightliner provided two daily services from Seaforth from the summer of 1979.

The nearby Containerbase depot at Aintree had previously benefited from the first ever Section 8 Grant, awarded in 1975. Further such grants enabled the upgrading of container-handling facilities at Ipswich and the refurbishment and improvement of facilities at Stratford Freightliner terminal, including the installation of a fifth track beneath the cranes. Freightliner was eligible for Section 8 funding at that time because it was not a BR subsidiary.

The trend towards taller maritime containers presented a problem for Freightliner because of the restricted loading gauge on most parts of the BR network. A major investment scheme to allow 8ft 6in containers to be carried on the East Coast Main Line involved lowering the track in Stoke, Peascliffe and Penmanshiel tunnels. The work was successfully completed at Stoke and Peascliffe, but Penmanshiel Tunnel collapsed during the project, causing the deaths of two construction workers, and the railway was rebuilt around the tunnel on a new alignment.

Under the 1978 Transport Act, control of Freightliner returned to the British Railways Board. This change was welcomed by many, although it also meant that Freightliner was no longer eligible to apply for Section 8 Grant funding. During the early 1980s the network of Freightliner terminals and services remained relatively stable, but the trend towards deep-sea traffic – and therefore away from domestic movements – was unrelenting. At Felixstowe traffic volumes outgrew the original rail terminal and a second facility, known as Felixstowe North, was opened in 1983. This terminal was initially reached by a port-owned siding connection from Felixstowe South, but in 1987 a new BR spur was opened allowing direct access from Trimley to Felixstowe North.

By 1985 the Freightliner network had reached its zenith, with more than 30 permanent terminals as listed in the accompanying table. However, the spread of business was uneven, with some regional terminals such as Dudley struggling to maintain viable volumes, and even the recently connected port terminal at Seaforth reduced to a single daily departure, connecting into various trunk services at nearby Garston. BR therefore set about pruning the network. The first casualties took effect in 1986 and included King's Cross, which latterly handled only a nightly Freightliner service to and from Edinburgh, and Dudley, whose traffic could easily be subsumed by the newer and better-equipped terminal at Birmingham Landor Street. The Containerbase terminal at Aintree and the Clydeport terminal at Greenock both closed to rail traffic, while the port of Harwich temporarily lost its container trains after Freightliner rerouted its European business via the Felixstowe to Zeebrugge crossing.

A more extensive cull of Freightliner terminals took place in April 1987. The axe fell on three out of the five Scottish terminals – Aberdeen, Dundee and Edinburgh – despite the potential for long-distance

Freightliner terminals, 1985		
Aberdeen	Barton Dock (Containerbase)	Dagenham
Dundee	Garston	(Dagenham Storage)
Coatbridge	Seaforth*	Tilbury*
Glasgow Gushetfaulds	Aintree (Containerbase)	Harwich*
Greenock*	Holyhead	Ipswich*
Edinburgh	Nottingham	Felixstowe South*
Newcastle	Birmingham Landor Street	Felixstowe North*
Stockton	Dudley	Cardiff Pengam
Leeds	Willesden	Swansea
Hull	King's Cross	Bristol
Longsight	Stratford	Southampton Millbrook
Trafford Park	Barking Ripple Lane	Southampton Maritime*
	*container port terminal	

Left Seaforth was connected to the rail system in 1979 in the hope of capturing new Freightliner business. No 47380 negotiates the Seaforth branch with 4F67, the 1740 departure to Garston, on 2 April 1986. The structure above the train was a rail loading facility for grain, which saw very little use.

Below No 47193 approaches Goose Hill Junction with 4O62, the 1836 Leeds to Southampton Freightliner train, on 14 July 1986. In the background lies the semi-derelict Normanton station, its broad island platform and extensive buildings recalling busier days.

Opposite top A Freightliner mini-terminal was established at Swindon to receive trainloads of New Zealand butter from Tilbury. Pilot locomotive No 08795 removes a

rake of wagons with empty containers from the loading area at Swindon on 31 July 1987, ready to form the 4E90 service to Tilbury in the early hours of the following morning. Freightliner also used Swindon to detach and attach a Bristol portion from/to the daily Stratford to Cardiff Pengam train.

Below In 1987 Southampton Millbrook Freightliner terminal handled three outward and four inward trains a day, most of which also called at Southampton Maritime. No 47189 leaves Millbrook with 4E85, the 1806 departure to Stratford, on 18 August 1987.

Left Aberdeen gained its Freightliner terminal in 1966. Unfortunately, despite the potential for long-distance flows to and from North East Scotland, loadings declined and Freightliner withdrew from the city in 1987. No 47117 passes Hilton Junction with a poorly loaded 4V37, the 1410 departure from Aberdeen to Glasgow, on 20 July 1984.

Below left Nottingham Beeston Freightliner terminal had an active life of just under 18 years before falling victim to the Freightliner cutbacks in April 1987. In later years wagons were tripped from Nottingham to Birmingham Landor Street to connect with trunk Freightliner trains. No 31167 departs from Nottingham with 4G50, the 1523 trip to Birmingham, on 27 July 1984.

Below right A regular Class 50 turn was 4A61, the 1808 Bristol West to Swindon Cocklebury Freightliner train. Network SouthEast-liveried locomotive No 50034 *Furious* passes Bristol East engineers' sidings with 4A61 on 30 July 1987. Freightliner withdrew from Bristol in 1992 following a review of its marginal business.

Right A drawback with the location of the Trafford Park complex is the need for trains to use the busy double-track corridor between Deansgate and Manchester Piccadilly. Still carrying InterCity livery, No 86410 approaches Manchester Piccadilly with 4E76, the 1314 Trafford Park to Tilbury Freightliner working, on 7 February 1987.

Below The extension of electrification to Coatbridge in 1981 cut out the need for a costly and time-consuming traction change at Mossend. Nos 87001 *Royal Scot* and 87016 pass Coatbridge Central station with 4V63, the 1805 Coatbridge to Cardiff Pengam train, on 12 July 1988. The load includes domestic curtain-sided containers as well as ISO boxes.

The driver of No 47050, in charge of 4M88, the 1346 Southampton to Willesden Freightliner train, chats to a member of the station staff at Eastleigh station while waiting for a relief crew on 19 August 1987.

One of the few tangible changes arising from the merger of Freightliner and Speedlink Distribution in 1988 was the use of the Speedlink network for low-volume Freightliner traffic between Bristol and Coatbridge. No 47079 approaches Dinmore Tunnel with 6S74, the 1954 Hereford to Coatbridge, on 9 July 1990, conveying vanloads of cider from Hereford as well as containers from Bristol.

hauls between these terminals and southern ports. Freightliner found it more cost-effective to serve the Scottish regions by road from Coatbridge. In England, Freightliner closed down five of its regional terminals: Newcastle, Hull, Longsight, Nottingham and Swansea. Much of the traffic using those terminals had been domestic rather than maritime.

The rearrangement of BR into business sectors in the late 1980s brought Freightliner under the control of Railfreight Distribution (RfD), the non-bulk arm of the BR freight business. Operationally, most Freightliner services continued to run separately from other freight flows; the only route where Freightliner regularly shared haulage with other RfD traffic was between Bristol and Coatbridge, where two Freightliner flats were

attached to scheduled Speedlink services via Gloucester and Warrington. A more noticeable change took place in traction policy, as regional allocations of locomotives gave way to sector-based groupings. From now on most Freightliner trains would be hauled by Freightliner locomotives, comprising members of Classes 37 and 47 based at Stratford, Classes 31 and 47 based at Crewe, and AC electric locomotives – mainly Class 86 – based at Willesden. A number of new Class 90 electrics were allocated to Freightliner from new, enabling some Anglo-Scottish Freightliner services to be hauled by a single locomotive in place of a pair of Class 86s.

The AC electrification of the North London line in 1988 made it possible for Freightliner to run electric-hauled trains between the West Coast Main Line and Tilbury, Harwich and Ipswich, obviating the need for locomotive changes in the London area. To begin with, only Ford company trains took advantage of the facility, but from May 1989 RfD diagrammed three pairs of Class 86 electrics on Freightliner services to and from East Anglia.

The following year, 1989, saw several changes to the Freightliner network. On Teesside the poorly sited Stockton facility was replaced by a new Freightliner terminal at Wilton, financed partly by an EEC grant. The new terminal was located within ICI's Teesside complex; this was useful not only because ICI was Freightliner's biggest customer in the region, but also because containers could

Nos 86410 and 86430 pass Camden Road with 4L75, the 0732 Garston to Felixstowe South Freightliner train, on 2 November 1989. The North London line had only recently gained its AC overhead electrification, but this photograph shows how the new gantries were grafted on to much older structures, installed back in the 1960s when the goods lines at this point had been electrified to provide access to York Way depot.

The port of Tilbury was home to an OCL mini-terminal, complementing the main Freightliner facility adjacent to the BR running line. No 08393 shunts a rake of Freightliner wagons between the two terminals on 6 July 1987.

be transported to and from local ICI installations without using public roads, which were then subject to a 38-tonne weight restriction, thereby allowing the containers to carry a heavier payload. Services from Wilton were heavily geared to the deep-sea market, with direct trains to Southampton and Felixstowe and connections available to Tilbury.

Freightliner services to Harwich were restored in 1989, allowing Felixstowe to concentrate on deep-sea business. The port of Immingham also gained a scheduled Freightliner connection, with a daily train to and from Leeds that also conveyed traffic between Immingham and Wilton. However, the Immingham service did not last

long, as too many of the boxes arriving there were destined for relatively local customers, for whom rail was not a viable option. A trial Freightliner service from Hull in the early 1990s was equally unsuccessful. On the western side of the country, some of Freightliner's Anglo-Irish business shifted from Holyhead to the Cawoods container terminal at Ellesmere Port in 1989, initially just two trains a week but later increasing to three daily trains.

An innovation for Freightliner in 1990 was the use of SNCF-registered 'Multifret' wagons with 90mph capability on services from Harwich. Their higher speed would not only produce shorter end-to-end journey times but would also

Trafford Park Freightliner depot opened in 1969 to supplement the original Manchester terminal at Longsight. No 86501 *Talyllyn – The First Preserved Railway*, one of the small batch of Class 86s then recently regeared for Freightliner traffic with a maximum speed of 75mph, departs from Trafford Park with a Southampton train on 28 January 1989.

Electric haulage was introduced on Freightliner trains to Ipswich and Harwich in 1989. Nos 86417 and 86438 pass Chadwell Heath with 4L88, the 1006 Willesden to Harwich Parkeston, on 4 July 1989.

Train movements to and from Felixstowe North became much easier once the direct spur to Trimley was opened in 1987. Nos 37154 and 37209 prepare to depart from Felixstowe North with 4S80, the 1943 Freightliner train to Coatbridge, on 10 July 1989.

reduce pathing conflicts with 100mph passenger expresses. Their low deck height of 945mm would also allow 9-foot-high containers and swapbodies to be carried on routes authorised for 8ft 6in containers on conventional wagons. In the event, the wagons were not authorised to run faster than 75mph in regular service and most workings carried only a handful of conventional containers; the service was therefore short-lived.

Leeds was one of the most successful inland Freightliner terminals, surviving the Freightliner cutbacks of the 1980s and still proving its worth in the 21st century. No 47307 backs into the Leeds terminal on 8 August 1989 after forming 4D79, the 1512 feeder service from Immingham. On the right is resident pilot locomotive No 08874.

Ellesmere Port became a short-term replacement for Holyhead for Anglo-Irish container traffic, with a twice-weekly service between Ellesmere Port and Crewe Basford Hall starting in 1989 and expanding to three daily trains in January 1990. No 47289 passes the Shell loading racks at Stanlow with 4K43, the 1419 from Ellesmere Port to Crewe, on 10 August 1989.

The Freightliner network was supplemented by feeder services to private sidings where suitable traffic was on offer. An example of this was the steel terminal at Round Oak, which received deliveries of cold reduced coil from Ipswich via a Freightliner feeder service from Birmingham Landor Street. No 47615 *Castell Caerffili/Caerphilly Castle* shunts a Freightliner set at Round Oak on 18 August 1989, having arrived on the 4T52 trip working.

Freightliner's increased use of Crewe Basford Hall yard as an interchange point led to the introduction of a trans-Pennine feeder service between Crewe and Leeds. No 31206 approaches Diggle with 4E51, the 0805 departure from Crewe, on 9 June 1990.

A more positive development was the ordering in 1990 of 700 new Freightliner wagons to replace the bulk of the first-generation FFA/FGA vehicles, many of which were reaching the end of their useful lives. BR placed the contract for the new wagons with the French company Arbel Fauvet and production started in 1991. The fleet was divided into 560 outer and 140 inner wagons, coded FSA and FTA respectively and semi-permanently coupled in two- and three-wagon sets. This arrangement gave greater flexibility for train operators than the five-wagon sets of FFA/FGA wagons. Freightliner by this time was also hiring a small fleet of Tiphook KFA container flats, which operated singly.

Freightliner added an important location to its deep-sea network in 1991 when a temporary rail terminal was opened at the new container port of Thamesport. Situated at the end of the 15-mile branch line from Hoo Junction to Grain, the facility made use of existing sidings and a mobile 40-tonne reach stacker. However, there was a major hurdle to overcome: clearances on the former South Eastern & Chatham Railway lines in North Kent were even tighter than on most other parts of the BR system and gauge enhancement work would be required before 8ft 6in containers could be carried there on Freightliner's existing wagons. By way of a short-term solution BR ordered a fleet of 45 wagons with a deck height of just 720mm, capable of carrying 8ft 6in containers to Thamesport and 9ft 6in containers on those routes cleared for 8ft 6in containers on conventional wagons. The new wagons, coded FLA, were built by Powell Duffryn Standard and entered service in the summer of 1991. BR was then able to launch a twice-daily shuttle service from Thamesport to Stratford. On arrival at Stratford the containers would be transhipped to standard wagons for the remainder of their journey. The longer-term solution was to increase clearances between Thamesport and

BR used French-registered 'Multifret' wagons to launch a 90mph intermodal service between Harwich and Garston in July 1990. No 90042 passes South Kenton with train 4M91, the 0945 departure from Harwich, on 2 November. Although 90mph operation was technically feasible, the experiment failed to demonstrate commercial viability and was short-lived.

London by lowering the track under eight overbridges. Once this work was completed, in 1993, Thamesport traffic could use standard wagons and the FLAs were redeployed to move 9ft 6in boxes throughout the system.

While deep-sea traffic blossomed, Freightliner was finding it increasingly hard to maintain its share of domestic business. The London terminals were vulnerable because the distance between London and the main deep-sea ports was relatively small, making the use of rail marginal. Willesden terminal, which had produced 11 daily Freightliner departures as recently as 1989, faced complete closure in 1992, with the site earmarked for redevelopment as a Channel Tunnel terminal. Stratford absorbed the residual traffic from Willesden, but not for long. Stratford lost its role as the transhipment point for Thamesport traffic once the Thamesport route became accessible to standard-height wagons in 1993 and its throughput was then reduced to just two trains a day, one serving Crewe with portions for four terminals in Northern England and Scotland, and the other serving the Hays distribution terminal at Dagenham. Stratford closed completely in 1994, its remaining rail business switching to Tilbury.

Another casualty of the reduced domestic business was Glasgow Gushetfaulds, whose remaining traffic was transferred to Coatbridge

Above **SNCF-liveried locomotive No 90130 *Fretconnection* heads north past Holme with an additional down Freightliner working on Saturday 10 October 1992.**

Below **Opened in 1965, Glasgow Gushetfaulds was the first Freightliner terminal in Scotland. It remained in use until 1993, when all Scottish Freightliner traffic was concentrated on Coatbridge. No 47249 shunts at Gushetfaulds on 13 July 1988 after arriving with 4S89, the 0425 departure from Willesden.**

in 1993. Gushetfaulds had latterly produced daily trunk departures to Willesden, Trafford Park and Harwich, plus feeder services to Coatbridge.

Freightliner's 23-year association with the North Wales Coast line came to an abrupt end in March 1991 when Sealink withdrew its freight sailings from Holyhead to Dublin and

Belfast. Initially all Irish Freightliner traffic was diverted to run via Ellesmere Port, which handled four daily services to and from Crewe by the end of the year. From 1992 the Irish business was transferred to Seaforth, feeding into Coastal Container Line sailings to Dublin and Belfast. This change provided a welcome boost for the Seaforth railhead, where substantial

yard as a portion exchange point for deep-sea traffic. Daily services operated between Crewe and all UK Freightliner terminals, so that almost any itinerary was possible with just one change of train. Among the less obvious journeys routed via Crewe were Thamesport to Cardiff and Tilbury to Birmingham; in neither case was there sufficient volume to support a direct

Seaforth container terminal produced reasonable volumes of Freightliner traffic in the 1990s, with some boxes conveyed by feeder services to and from Garston in addition to direct trunk trains. Trainload Coal locomotive No 37222 leaves Seaforth with the lunchtime train to Garston on 30 October 1992.

improvements had been carried out in 1991 including the lengthening of the two existing sidings and the provision of a third.

A major recasting of the Freightliner network was carried out in May 1992, followed by some fine-tuning in January and May 1993. The result was to enhance the role of Crewe Basford Hall

trainload service. Crewe also became the focal point for RfD's electric traction diagrams, with many trains hauled by a pair of Class 86s north of Crewe and a single Class 90 south of Crewe. This arrangement provided the optimum haulage for a 1,250-tonne train over the differing gradient profiles of the northern and southern sections of the West Coast Main Line. A few trains were hauled by a pair of Class 86s south of Crewe to enable their load to be increased to 1,600 tonnes.

On non-electrified routes RfD opted for Class 47 haulage on most services, including almost all Freightliner workings. Pairs of Class 37s had been introduced in 1991 on the heaviest trains out of Southampton, but they turned out to be less reliable than the 47s, and the need for double-heading was also expensive. However, double-headed Class 37s continued to operate between Felixstowe and Ipswich, where they could haul a 1,600-tonne train compared with the 980-tonne threshold for a single Class 47 locomotive.

Class 37 haulage was also necessary to comply with route availability constraints on the West Highland line, where Freightliner at that time carried paper reels from Corpach and aluminium ingots from Fort William.

The mid-1990s were a time of uncertainty for Freightliner as Britain's railways passed into the

Freightliner timetable, March 1995					
Code	Dep	Days	From	To	Also detaches or attaches traffic at
4L69	0018	MX	Birmingham	Felixstowe	Wembley
4O18	0333	MX	Birmingham	Southampton MCT	
4O26	1210	SO	Birmingham	Southampton MCT	
4K50	2000	SX	Birmingham	Crewe Basford Hall	
4E68	0720	MX	Cardiff Pengam	Lynemouth	
4S81	1820	SX	Cardiff Pengam	Coatbridge	Crewe
4S81	1830	SuO	Cardiff Pengam	Coatbridge	Mossend
4M68	1946	SX	Cardiff Pengam	Crewe Basford Hall	
4O33	2040	FO	Cardiff Pengam	Southampton MCT	
4O27	0500	MX	Coatbridge	Southampton MCT	Crewe, Millbrook (MSX)
4O32	1114	SO	Coatbridge	Southampton MCT	
4L60	1530	SX	Coatbridge	Felixstowe	Crewe
4V63	1819	SX	Coatbridge	Cardiff Pengam	Crewe
4L81	1859	SX	Coatbridge	Tilbury	Crewe
4L58	1945	SX	Coatbridge	Felixstowe	Crewe
4L95	2121	SX	Coatbridge	Felixstowe	Crewe
4M81	2324	SX	Coatbridge	Seaforth	Crewe
7D19	0951	SX	Corpach	Mossend	Fort William, Coatbridge
4G57	0039	MX	Crewe Basford Hall	Birmingham	
4V04	0043	MO	Crewe Basford Hall	Cardiff Pengam	
4V04	0150	MX	Crewe Basford Hall	Cardiff Pengam	
4E53	0245	MX	Crewe Basford Hall	Leeds	
4L91	0426	MX	Crewe Basford Hall	Tilbury	
4O86	0640	SO	Crewe Basford Hall	Thamesport	
4S50	0705	MX	Crewe Basford Hall	Coatbridge	
4O86	0816	MSX	Crewe Basford Hall	Thamesport	
4E52	1920	SX	Crewe Basford Hall	Leeds	
4H58	2053	SX	Crewe Basford Hall	Trafford Park	
4M62	2120	SX	Dagenham	Wembley	Tilbury
4B50	1652	FO	Didcot	Cardiff Pengam	

Freightliner timetable, March 1995

4M45	0229	MX	Felixstowe	Trafford Park	
4S87	0821	SX	Felixstowe	Coatbridge	Crewe
4M47	1132	SX	Felixstowe	Garston	Crewe
4S88	1651	SX	Felixstowe	Coatbridge	Crewe
4E50	1732	SX	Felixstowe	Wilton	Leeds
4M87	1820	SX	Felixstowe	Trafford Park	Crewe
4M53	2042	SX	Felixstowe	Trafford Park	
4M73	2225	SX	Felixstowe	Garston	
4M35	2308	SX	Felixstowe	Birmingham	Wembley
7Y31	0710	SX	Fort William	Corpach	
4O21	0230	MX	Garston	Southampton MCT	Crewe, Millbrook
4F74	0800	SO	Garston	Seaforth	
4F74	1227	MSX	Garston	Seaforth	
4L71	1924	SX	Garston	Felixstowe	
4O11	2145	SX	Garston	Millbrook	Crewe
4L89	0030	MSX	Leeds	Felixstowe	Crewe
4L89	0030	SO	Leeds	Felixstowe	
4O31	1509	SO	Leeds	Southampton MCT	
4O07	1828	SX	Leeds	Southampton MCT	
4L63	2020	SX	Leeds	Tilbury	
4M21	2320	SX	Leeds	Crewe Basford Hall	
4V03	1958	SX	Lynemouth	Cardiff Pengam	
8B01	0643	MX	Millbrook	Southampton MCT	
4S59	1303	SX	Millbrook	Coatbridge	Crewe
4B01	1844	SX	Millbrook	Southampton MCT	
4M79	1955	SX	Millbrook	Birmingham	
7Y45	0915	SX	Mossend	Fort William	Coatbridge
4O09	0248	MO	Ripple Lane	Southampton MCT	
4O09	0335	MX	Ripple Lane	Southampton MCT	
4O25	1335	EWD	Ripple Lane	Southampton MCT	
4K53	1126	SO	Seaforth	Crewe Basford Hall	
4K58	1426	SX	Seaforth	Crewe Basford Hall	Garston
4K67	1739	SX	Seaforth	Crewe Basford Hall	
4L62	0510	SO	Southampton MCT	Ripple Lane	
4L66	0800	SX	Southampton MCT	Ripple Lane	
8B02	0835	MX	Southampton MCT	Millbrook	
4S55	0900	FO	Southampton MCT	Coatbridge	Didcot, Crewe
4S55	0900	FSX	Southampton MCT	Coatbridge	Birmingham, Crewe
4M60	1309	SO	Southampton MCT	Birmingham	

INTERMODAL

Freightliner timetable, March 1995					
4M99	1716	SX	Southampton MCT	Trafford Park	Crewe
4S59	1812	SuO	Southampton MCT	Coatbridge	Mossend
4M40	1915	SX	Southampton MCT	Garston	Millbrook, Crewe
4E76	1948	SX	Southampton MCT	Leeds	
4E76	2016	SuO	Southampton MCT	Leeds	Crewe
4L78	2112	SuO	Southampton MCT	Ripple Lane	
4L78	2204	SX	Southampton MCT	Ripple Lane	
4M58	2304	SuO	Southampton MCT	Trafford Park	
4M58	2311	SX	Southampton MCT	Trafford Park	
4L87	1805	SX	Swindon	Tilbury	
4M49	1754	SX	Thamesport	Crewe Basford Hall	
4M96	1937	SX	Thamesport	Trafford Park	Crewe
4M54	1221	SX	Tilbury	Crewe Basford Hall	
4V15	1347	SX	Tilbury	Swindon	
4S83	1832	SX	Tilbury	Coatbridge	Crewe
4M37	2041	SX	Tilbury	Garston	Crewe
4E65	2330	SX	Tilbury	Leeds	
4L83	0015	MX	Trafford Park	Felixstowe	Crewe
4O22	0325	MX	Trafford Park	Southampton MCT	Crewe
4K04	1110	SO	Trafford Park	Crewe Basford Hall	
4O30	1347	SO	Trafford Park	Southampton MCT	
4O84	1810	SX	Trafford Park	Thamesport	Crewe
4L98	2032	SX	Trafford Park	Tilbury	Crewe
4O08	2115	SX	Trafford Park	Southampton MCT	
4L82	2231	FO	Trafford Park	Felixstowe	
4L82	2325	FSX	Trafford Park	Felixstowe	
4L50	0441	MX	Wembley	Dagenham	
4L79	1613	SX	Wilton	Felixstowe	Leeds

With several Tiphook KQA 'pocket' wagons in tow, Railfreight Distribution-liveried locomotive No 47292 passes Millbrook in charge of 4E74, the 1225 Southampton Maritime to Leeds Freightliner train, on 20 July 1998.

Charterail

A Charterail trailer is backed on to a 'Piggyback' wagon in Melton Mowbray goods yard on 27 August 1991.

Bi-modal transport, where a complete road trailer is carried on rail wheels, had an inauspicious history in the UK. As early as the 1960s attempts were made to introduce the American 'Roadrailer' system to Britain's railways but, although a complete Roadrailer train was built and passed for UK operation, it never turned a wheel in revenue-earning service.

Two decades later, the enterprising company Charterail made a fresh attempt to make bi-modal transport work, using specially designed 'Piggyback' trailers and wagons. The equipment was used first to carry trainloads of petfood from the Pedigree factory at Melton Mowbray to distribution railheads at Cricklewood and Deanside. The first loaded movements to Cricklewood took place in February 1991. Charterail later introduced a nightly 'Piggyback' service for the general distribution market between Cricklewood, Warrington and Deanside.

For its 'Piggyback' services Charterail leased a fleet of 100 wagons, coded KOA for TOPS purposes, from Tiphook. Each wagon had a hinged central section that could be swung out in order for a road trailer to be backed on to it, then moved back into the main body of the wagon and secured for transit.

A similar procedure enabled unloading at the destination. A mobile hydraulic power unit was required to activate the air suspension of the trailers before unloading,

The short length of the sidings in Melton Mowbray goods yard meant that several shunts were necessary to load a complete train of 'Piggyback' vehicles. Initially a Class 08 shunter was used, but later this was swapped for a Class 20 locomotive. No 20195 is in charge on 2 January 1992.

and a retractable lifting beam held the weight of the trailer while a road tractor unit drew up to it. The Charterail curtain-sided trailers were rather smaller than standard road trailers because they had to fit within the BR loading gauge when loaded on to the wagons.

Charterail had a dual relationship with BR: it hired BR (Railfreight Distribution) locomotives and crews to haul its trains, and 22% of its shares were owned by the British Railways Board. The main incentive for Pedigree and other customers to use Charterail was that they could dispense with warehousing at the destination end of the rail journey, as the trailers could switch from rail to road haulage in less than 10 minutes ready for their final delivery to the customer. However, the rail end of the operation was quite labour-intensive. The track layout at Melton Mowbray did not allow a full 30-wagon train to be loaded at once, so BR had to provide a Class 08 or Class 20 pilot locomotive to move short rakes of wagons between the loading area and the Up Loop, from where the train would eventually depart.

While the Pedigree traffic gave Charterail an assured volume of business, the expansion into general freight distribution was much riskier. Nevertheless, Charterail gained the support of some 13 companies, including Safeway and Heinz, to set up its initial route linking Cricklewood, Warrington and Deanside. The service was officially launched by the Transport Secretary in June 1992. At Warrington the company used the former BR Dallam freight terminal, conveniently

located beside the West Coast Main Line. Charterail planned eventually to expand the operation to about a dozen locations, including Wakefield, Avonmouth, Plymouth, Aberdeen, Birmingham and South London.

Unfortunately, the Charterail experiment came to an abrupt end in August 1992. The company claimed that its new style of integrating road and rail distribution had worked but that it could not afford BR's haulage charges and was unable to compete with road-based distribution. The poor state of the national economy at that time did not help. The collapse of one of the biggest private users of Britain's rail network on the eve of rail privatisation was unfortunate to say the least, but there was no prospect of saving Charterail, and the 'Piggyback' concept was, again, discredited.

After the collapse it was difficult to find any further use for the fleet of 100 'Piggyback' wagons and 80 trailers. In 1997 a single KOA wagon was modified with a generator and compressor and used to power a set of Autoballaster wagons for railway infrastructure work. In the following year Freightliner reinstated some KOAs to run a 'Piggyback' service for Exel tank containers between Tilbury and Garston. But neither of these ventures was successful and by 2000 the entire fleet of Charterail rolling-stock was consigned to the scrapyard.

Just a few days before the collapse of Charterail, No 47376 backs out of Deanside on 11 August 1992 with the overnight 'flyer' to Cricklewood.

Once the permanent container terminal at Thamesport was open, Freightliner services to and from the port increased, reaching four trains a day by 1998. Gauge clearance in North Kent had allowed standard wagons to carry 8ft 6in boxes, while low-deck vehicles including KQA 'pocket' wagons could now be used to carry 9ft 6in containers to and from the port. Nos 47204 and 47361 are pictured arriving at Thamesport on 22 July 1998 with a mixed rake of FLA and KQA wagons, having formed 4O88, the 2333 departure from Leeds.

Crewe Basford Hall sidings became a busy node on the Freightliner network, as well as handling large amounts of infrastructure traffic for Freightliner Heavy Haul. No 57007 waits in No 2 Up Arrival siding with 4O29, the 1415 Trafford Park to Southampton train, on 8 August 2000.

Doncaster Railport did not attract any regular Channel Tunnel traffic, but was used by various deep-sea and domestic intermodal flows, including a daily trainload of containerised chemicals from Wilton. No 47231 backs into the Railport siding at Doncaster on 29 May 1998 after working 4D87, the 1148 departure from Wilton.

synergies with Channel Tunnel traffic. Freightliner was reported at that time to be losing £3 million a month.

private sector. Freightliner was offered for sale separately from the rest of RfD. The American-led consortium that bought most of Britain's rail freight operations to form English Welsh & Scottish Railways (EWS) was not interested in Freightliner, despite the significant recent investment in new rolling-stock and the possible

EWS launched its Enterprise feeder service to Grangemouth in 1997, providing a useful intermodal railhead for the chemical industries in the Grangemouth district. No 37427 positions a KFA wagon in the Grangemouth port terminal after working 6N34, the 0840 departure from Mossend, on 16 July 1998.

In the event, it was a brave management buy-out that took ownership of Freightliner in May 1996. The early results were encouraging: the number of boxes carried rose from 462,000 in 1995/96 to 490,000 in 1996/97, and company's deficit in 1996/97 was actually £3.4 million compared with an expected figure of £5 million. Nevertheless, much work needed to be done to place the business on a firm long-term footing.

Despite the apparently poor performance of Freightliner, other companies showed interest in carrying containers by rail once the market was opened up through privatisation. Mainline Freight, one of the three companies resulting

from the pre-privatisation carve-up of BR Trainload Freight, launched an intermodal service from Harwich to the new European distribution terminal at Doncaster in 1995. This service was later developed by EWS as a joint venture with Combined Transport Limited (CTL) and Stena Line, using CTL 'Multifret' wagons.

Meanwhile Freightliner's top priority was to maintain, and if possible increase, its 30% operating gear and air cylinders mounted above the bogies at opposite ends of the wagon and a 40-foot-long central 'pocket' for the load. The 'pocket' wagons had a deck height of just 475mm above rail level, which was lower than any other British

In the heyday of the EWS Enterprise network, containers were carried on numerous routes for both maritime and domestic customers. No 56067 leaves Doncaster Belmont yard on 25 April 2001 with an additional 6Z31 1045 departure to Warrington Arpley, conveying boxes for Liverpool Seaforth.

The O'Connor Group set up its intermodal railhead on the former British Oxygen Company site at Widnes during 1998. Initially, the terminal was served by EWS intermodal and Enterprise trains to and from Harwich, Warrington and Mossend. A direct service to Immingham also ran for a time. Hunslet 0-6-0 No 7189 stands coupled to one of the then newly delivered IKA 'Megafret' twin wagons at Widnes on 11 December 1998.

The Far North line freight revival continued into the 21st century with Safeway container traffic to Georgemas Junction. No 66098 stands at Britain's most northerly railway junction on 21 August 2001 with a mixed load of Safeway intermodal traffic and VGA vans. Unfortunately, the Far North revival could not be sustained and soon all that remained was the weekly oil train to Lairg. *Gavin Morrison*

wagon type, but the downside was that they were 68 feet long, with 28 feet of unproductive length.

In 1998 Freightliner launched an experimental 'Piggyback' service for Exel Logistics, conveying specially built road semi-trailers of chemicals between Trafford Park and Tilbury. The service used some of the former Charterail KOA bi-modal wagons, now owned by Tiphook. Unfortunately the experiment was short-lived.

As well as updating its wagon fleet, Freightliner needed to develop a motive power strategy that would take the company forward into the 21st century. The Class 47 locomotives inherited from BR were now around 40 years old; Freightliner had had to hire in Class 56 locomotives from EWS and Class 37s from Direct Rail Services to supplement its own fleet. In 1997 Freightliner commissioned the total rebuilding of six of its Class 47s with reconditioned General Motors 645 power units, reworked ex-Class 56 alternator groups and new cab interiors. The work was undertaken by Brush at Loughborough and the first of the 'new' locomotives, designated Class 57, entered service in the summer of 1998. The arrival of No 57001 gave Freightliner the opportunity to launch its new two-tone green livery.

Freightliner scored a major success in 1998 when it clinched a five-year contract with its existing customer P&O Nedlloyd to move up to 40,000 40-foot containers annually from Southampton. Freightliner's carryings from Felixstowe also showed significant growth, reaching a record total of 250,000 containers in 1998. The Port of Felixstowe received a Freight Facilities Grant of more than £1.8 million towards the cost of additional craneage and rail terminal infrastructure, so that it could increase its rail throughput to 280,000 containers by 2001. Freightliner itself received Freight Facilities Grant funding of £1.35 million in 1998, enabling it to install new cranes at Trafford Park as well as contributing to the cost of 40 additional KTA 'pocket' wagons for 9ft 6in containers. Some of the pressure on Trafford Park was relieved in early 1998 when Freightliner opened a mini-terminal within its Basford Hall yard complex at Crewe. The company also commissioned its own locomotive fuelling point at Basford Hall in 1998.

Although the deep-sea side of the business became ever more dominant, Freightliner continued to develop European and domestic flows where possible. It added Purfleet to its network in 1997, connecting with Cobelfret sailings to and from Belgium. It arranged the long-term hire of a European Passenger Services Class 37 locomotive in order to keep Alcan ingot traffic from Fort William on the rails. And it won a three-year contract to move container-loads of nylon polymer from Wilton to Doncaster for DuPont Nylon, a distance of just 92 miles. This flow provided useful extra business for the under-utilised terminal at Wilton and was the first regular Freightliner train to serve Doncaster Railport.

While Freightliner saw its traffic grow, the company's near-monopoly status in the intermodal business was now open to challenge from other operators. EWS entered the market by using its Enterprise network to carry containers in less-than-trainload quantities, initially avoiding direct competition with Freightliner but nonetheless paving the way for Freightliner-style services to and from the major container ports in the future.

The first movement of maritime boxes by scheduled Enterprise services took place in August 1997, when EWS, the Tees & Hartlepool Port Authority and P&O North Sea Ferries opened an intermodal railhead at Teesport. The volume of railborne containers at Teesport rose sharply and reached 160 units a week by the end of 1998. Most of the traffic ran to and from Scottish terminals at Mossend Eurocentral, Glasgow Deanside, Grangemouth and Aberdeen. The Grangemouth facility had been opened by Forth Ports in March 1997. Teesport also became the rail loading point for 5,000 tank containers

Two prototype Eurospine wagon sets entered service in 1998 carrying Parcelforce trailers between Willesden and Mossend, running northbound as part of a combined intermodal and automotive train and southbound as a dedicated working. One of the specially adapted Parcelforce trailers is lifted at Mossend Euroterminal on 15 July 1998.

Carcasses from the aftermath of the 2000/01 foot and mouth outbreak were conveyed by Freightliner to Calvert landfill site. No 47349 arrives at Oxford Hinksey yard with 4Z70, the 1000 Crewe to Calvert train, on 23 July 2001. EWS also carried a share of this traffic.

Warrington Dallam freight depot was the railhead for a short-term intermodal flow to and from Glasgow Deanside, using mobile lifting equipment, which obviated the need for an expensive gantry crane. No 56110 waits at Dallam on 1 August 2001 before forming train 4Z59, the 1129 departure to Deanside.

The TDG intermodal terminal at Grangemouth was served initially by Freightliner but later switched to EWS as Freightliner concentrated on point-to-point trainloads of deep sea traffic. No 66096 waits at Grangemouth on 27 August 2003 before departing with train 4M67, the 1801 to Trafford Park. This train was later amended to serve Mossend instead of Grangemouth, enabling the mothballing of the Grangemouth terminal.

a year, containing pure terephthalic acid bound for Workington, a much prized flow that EWS gained in the spring of 1998.

The growing Enterprise network enabled EWS to compete for intermodal traffic to and from Immingham, Hull and Purfleet – locations that Freightliner had also tried to serve but where the traffic on offer was better suited to wagonload than trainload operation. A further expansion of EWS intermodal services took place in the autumn of 1998, when new trunk trains were introduced linking Harwich with Newport Docks, Widnes and Liverpool Seaforth, together with a feeder service linking Widnes

and Liverpool Seaforth with Warrington Arpley. Widnes was a new location for intermodal traffic and would soon boast two rail-served facilities, one operated by O'Connors on the site of the former British Oxygen Company factory, and the other operated by AHC on an adjacent site. Further new railheads for intermodal traffic were opened at Plymouth Friary and Swansea Docks.

In March 1999 EWS launched a high-profile intermodal service for the high street retailer Safeway, carrying foodstuffs in refrigerated swapbodies from Mossend to Inverness. The service was later extended to Georgemas Junction, feeding Safeway stores in Caithness and in the

RAILFREIGHT: CONTAINERS, CARS AND SPECIAL TRAFFICS

Orkney Islands. Unfortunately the service was to come to an untimely end in 2004 after Morrisons took over Safeway and sold some of its stores to Tesco.

The rolling-stock for EWS's first intermodal services comprised a mixture of 'Multifret' (FIA/IFA), Tiphook (KFA) and ex-Freightliner (FFA/FGA) wagons. These types were able to carry containers up to 8ft 6in high on most routes. Like Freightliner, EWS needed to cater for the rising number of 9-foot and 9ft 6in boxes. It therefore included a tranche of 100 FAA well wagons with a deck height of 712mm in its Thrall Car building programme, for delivery in 1999. Thrall Car also supplied EWS with 400 FCA wagons with a deck height of 1023mm and 300 FKA wagons with a deck height of 820mm, enabling the company to cater efficiently for a range of different box sizes. The ex-Freightliner cast-offs and other older stock would gradually be phased out.

Undaunted by the failure of the Charterail 'Piggyback' system, EWS pressed ahead with two bi-modal experiments, using specially designed rolling-stock to carry complete road trailers. In 1998 the company took delivery of two prototype sets of KDA Eurospine wagons, built by Thrall Car, and used them to carry Parcelforce trailers between Willesden Euroterminal and Mossend. The second scheme used prototype 'Roadrailer' vehicles to carry paper from Aberdeen to Northampton. Unfortunately, neither of these experiments stood the commercial test of time. The Parcelforce traffic finished in 2002 and plans to build 20 more Eurospine sets were quietly forgotten.

While EWS made its entry into the deep-sea business, Freightliner continued to strengthen its own provision for maritime flows. In 1999 it added three terminals to its network: Widnes O'Connors, which was served initially by a trip from Garston; Hams Hall, which was served by a Felixstowe to Birmingham train; and Tilbury International Rail Freight Terminal, which took some of the pressure off Tilbury Freightliner terminal. In the same year Freightliner received six additional Class 57 locomotives, bringing the fleet total to 12, as well as its first order for Class 66s, which arrived in July. The £36 million investment in locomotives was complemented by some £4.5 million spent on new road tractor units for use at Freightliner's regional terminals. The Class 66 locomotives were an immediate success; further orders followed and would enable the phasing out of Freightliner's Class 47s – and, in due course, its Class 57s as well.

GB Railfreight successfully built up a portfolio of intermodal trains from Felixstowe, serving inland terminals at Selby, Doncaster and Hams Hall. No 66712 passes Ely with 6L72, the 1200 Hams Hall to Felixstowe train, on 17 July 2002.

The Howgill Fells form an imposing backdrop as Direct Rail Services loco No 66409 passes Docker with 4M44, the 0821 Mossend to Daventry Malcolms train, on 13 February 2008.

As the new century dawned, Freightliner's business continued to grow, with 13% more containers carried in 1999/2000 than in the previous year. In October 2000 Freightliner operated the first revenue-earning train from the new TDG container terminal at Grangemouth, built mainly to handle powders and liquids from the adjacent BP Chemicals plant. However, the Grangemouth traffic did not fit well into Freightliner's trainload plan and in 2001 its operation switched to EWS, which provided daily block trains to and from Trafford Park and Daventry, together with a feeder service to and from Mossend for less-than-trainload business. In South Wales the long-established Pengam Freightliner terminal was replaced in February 2001 by a new facility at Wentloog, offering twice the capacity of its predecessor. Wentloog was served initially by a direct train to Felixstowe and by a feeder train to Crewe for connections to

other destinations.

In 2001/02 Freightliner faced yet more competition in the intermodal business. Direct Rail Services (DRS) launched a Grangemouth to Daventry service in conjunction with logistics firm W. H. Malcolm, initially using pairs of its own Class 37 locomotives but later switching to Class 66s hired from GB Railfreight while its own fleet of Class 66s was on order. The Daventry to Scotland corridor proved to be fertile ground for DRS, with five trains a day in each direction operating by 2008.

Meanwhile GB Railfreight (GBRf) signed a five-year contract with the Medite Shipping Corporation for deep-sea traffic between Felixstowe and Selby, starting in February 2002, followed two months later by a new service from Felixstowe to Hams Hall. By September GBRf was running a daily train on each route, using its newly acquired Class 66 locomotives. Initially GBRf carried the containers on FCA intermodal wagons hired from EWS, but they were soon replaced by purpose-built FEA flats. GBRf would later increase its Felixstowe to Hams Hall service

Wakefield Euroterminal never established itself as a Channel Tunnel railhead but began to thrive as EWS entered the deep-sea container market. A visit to Wakefield on 18 February 2004 finds No 66152 in charge of 6E45, the 0301 departure from Felixstowe, and No 66077 with 6E98, the 0330 from Wembley. In 2010 Wakefield gained additional traffic following the closure of DB Schenker's Trafford Park terminal.

to three trains a day and would also introduce a train from Felixstowe to Doncaster Railport.

Freightliner's strategy was now to consolidate its business on core routes and make its operations as streamlined as possible. In 2002 the company scaled down its 'hub and spoke' operation centred on Basford Hall yard, Crewe, and reverted to running block trains directly between ports and individual regional terminals. Freightliner had already withdrawn from two of its least productive locations – Purfleet and Fort William – and reduced its service from Seaforth to one train a day. On the positive side, the company signed a major three-year contract with P&O Nedlloyd, complementing an earlier deal agreed with OOCL.

EWS was now well established in the intermodal business and, with its Enterprise wagonload network facing cutbacks, it concentrated on developing trainload

flows. In 2003 it launched the product Intermodal Express, which covered flows from Felixstowe to Widnes and Wakefield; Southampton to Hams Hall, Widnes and Wakefield; Thamesport to Widnes; and Hams Hall to Glasgow Deanside

Freightliner timetable, January 2004					
Code	Dep	Days	From	To	Also detaches or attaches traffic at
4L69	0040	SO	Birmingham	Ipswich (for FS*)	
4L69	0110	MSX	Birmingham	Ipswich (for FS*)	
4L84	0213	SO	Birmingham	Tilbury	
4L84	0250	MSX	Birmingham	Tilbury	
4O18	0444	MSX	Birmingham	Southampton MCT	
4O18	0705	MO	Birmingham	Southampton MCT	
4L90	0840	SO	Birmingham	Ipswich (for FN*)	
4L93	0942	MSX	Birmingham	Ipswich (for FS*)	
4O02	0959	SO	Birmingham	Southampton MCT	
4O17	1551	SX	Birmingham	Southampton MCT	
4L77	2305	SX	Birmingham	Ipswich (for FN*)	
4M27	0500	MX	Coatbridge	Crewe Basford Hall	
4O11	1852	SX	Coatbridge	Southampton MCT	Crewe
4L81	1930	SX	Coatbridge	Tilbury	Crewe
4L89	2200	SX	Coatbridge	Ipswich (for FN*)	
4L92	1330	SX	Ditton	Ipswich (for FN*)	Crewe
4L71	1830	SX	Ditton	Ipswich (for FS*)	
* FS = Felixstowe South, FN = Felixstowe North				*Table continues…*	

– catering almost exclusively for deep-sea traffic. Alongside its business with Freightliner, P&O Nedlloyd contracted EWS with up to 10,000 container movements a year, mainly from Southampton. In 2002 EWS had carried out trials for P&O Nedlloyd with a 90mph service between Willesden and Mossend, achieving a journey time of 5hr 30min; however, plans to run regular 90mph intermodal trains were shelved because the benefits of a shorter journey time were outweighed by the reduced axle loading – and therefore lower payload – incurred by the higher speed.

EWS's strategy of targeting trainload intermodal business resulted in 60% more boxes being carried in January 2003 than six months previously, with some record tonnages handled at individual terminals such as Wakefield and Mossend. Further gains included traffic for Argos and Ikea on routes such as Southampton to Burton-on-Trent and Felixstowe to Ely. However, some planned additions to the network did not materialise, such as Stranraer, where gradients on the line of route meant that viable volumes could not be carried.

A challenge for all intermodal operators was the growing proportion of 9ft 6in-high containers arriving at deep-sea ports, reaching one in four by 2004 and expected to rise further in the years ahead. The use of low-deck wagons provided a short-term solution on some routes, but Freightliner and other intermodal operators regarded loading gauge

Freightliner timetable, January 2004 (Continued)

4L91	0205	SO	Garston	Tilbury	
4L67	0330	MSX	Garston	Tilbury	
4O14	0432	MX	Garston	Southampton MCT	
4L60	1954	SX	Garston	Ipswich (for FS*)	
4L90	1417	SX	Hams Hall	Ipswich (for FS*)	Daventry
4M47	0120	SO	Ipswich (from FN*)	Hams Hall	Daventry
4M52	0222	MSX	Ipswich (from FN*)	Hams Hall	Daventry
4E58	0343	MX	Ipswich (from FN*)	Leeds	
4M45	0348	MX	Ipswich (from FN*)	Ditton	Crewe
4R90	0944	SO	Ipswich (from FN*)	Tilbury	
4R90	1015	MSX	Ipswich (from FN*)	Tilbury	
4M81	1044	MO	Ipswich (from FN*)	Trafford Park	
4M87	1249	SX	Ipswich (from FN*)	Trafford Park	
4M93	1516	SX	Ipswich (from FN*)	Birmingham	
4S88	1825	SX	Ipswich (from FN*)	Coatbridge	
4E60	2023	SX	Ipswich (from FN*)	Wilton	
4M53	2154	SX	Ipswich (from FN*)	Trafford Park	
4M42	2325	SX	Ipswich (from FN*)	Garston	
4M86	0455	SX	Ipswich (from FS*)	Birmingham	
4M81	1044	MSX	Ipswich (from FS*)	Trafford Park	
4V30	1843	SX	Ipswich (from FS*)	Wentloog	
4E50	1845	SX	Ipswich (from FS*)	Leeds	
4M92	2006	SX	Ipswich (from FS*)	Birmingham	
4M73	2308	SX	Ipswich (from FS*)	Ditton	
4L83	0235	MX	Leeds	Ipswich (for FS*)	
4O54	0548	SO	Leeds	Southampton MCT	
4O54	0551	MSX	Leeds	Millbrook	
4L85	0858	MSX	Leeds	Ipswich (for FS*)	
4L85	0858	SO	Leeds	Ipswich (for FN*)	
4N01	1022	SX	Leeds	Wilton	
4O31	1058	SO	Leeds	Southampton MCT	
4O31	1800	SX	Leeds	Millbrook	
4L63	2012	SX	Leeds	Tilbury	
4O07	2027	SX	Leeds	Southampton MCT	
4E01	0214	MSX	Millbrook	Leeds	
4V50	0503	MSX	Millbrook	Wentloog	
4E44	0845	SX	Millbrook	Leeds	
8B05	0905	SX	Millbrook	Southampton MCT	
8B08	1548	SX	Millbrook	Southampton MCT	

* FS = Felixstowe South, FN = Felixstowe North   *Table continues…*

Freightliner timetable, January 2004 (Continued)					
4E76	2014	SX	Millbrook	Leeds	
4O09	0509	SO	Ripple Lane	Southampton MCT	
4R65	1702	SX	Ripple Lane	Tilbury	
4O32	1846	FSX	Ripple Lane	Southampton MCT	
4K58	1532	SX	Seaforth	Crewe Basford Hall	
4E01	0010	MO	Southampton MCT	Leeds	
4L78	0032	MX	Southampton MCT	Ripple Lane	
4M95	0343	SO	Southampton MCT	Birmingham	
4M95	0343	SX	Southampton MCT	Trafford Park	
4V50	0503	MO	Southampton MCT	Wentloog	
8B04	0730	SX	Southampton MCT	Millbrook	
4M55	0951	SO	Southampton MCT	Birmingham	
4M55	1012	SX	Southampton MCT	Birmingham	
8B06	1047	SX	Southampton MCT	Millbrook	
8B06	1133	SO	Southampton MCT	Millbrook	
4M61	1252	SX	Southampton MCT	Trafford Park	
4S59	1524	SX	Southampton MCT	Coatbridge	
4M99	1624	SX	Southampton MCT	Trafford Park	
4M98	1824	SX	Southampton MCT	Garston	
4M58	1920	SuO	Southampton MCT	Trafford Park	

enhancement as essential if rail was to maintain its market share in the longer term. During 2004 the Strategic Rail Authority funded a £30 million upgrade of the Felixstowe to Birmingham corridor via London to W10 gauge, enabling 9ft 6in boxes to be carried on standard-deck wagons to locations such as Daventry, Hams Hall and

Diesel haulage under the wires became the norm for intermodal traffic between Southampton and the North West, as this was a more cost-effective option than changing locomotives at Willesden or Bescot. No 66536 heads north at Rugeley with 4M58, the 1028 Southampton to Crewe Freightliner train, on 23 July 2009.

Freightliner timetable, January 2004 (Continued)					
4E76	2020	SuO	Southampton MCT	Leeds	
4M40	2034	SX	Southampton MCT	Trafford Park	
4M79	2257	FSX	Southampton MCT	Birmingham	
4L86	1039	SX	Thamesport	Tilbury	
4M57	2115	SX	Thamesport	Trafford Park	
4Y79	0520	MX	Tilbury	Ipswich (for FN*)	
4O87	0803	SO	Tilbury	Thamesport	
4O87	1026	MSX	Tilbury	Thamesport	
4R60	1530	SX	Tilbury	Ripple Lane	
4S83	1828	SX	Tilbury	Coatbridge	Crewe
4M39	1750	SX	Tilbury	Birmingham	
4M37	2135	SX	Tilbury	Garston	
4E65	2258	SX	Tilbury	Leeds	
4O22	0109	SO	Trafford Park	Southampton MCT	
4O22	0125	MSX	Trafford Park	Southampton MCT	
4K67	0210	MSX	Trafford Park	Crewe Basford Hall	
4L97	0457	MSX	Trafford Park	Ipswich (for FS*)	
4L97	0501	SO	Trafford Park	Ipswich (for FN*)	
4O27	0514	MX	Trafford Park	Southampton MCT	
4L93	0822	SO	Trafford Park	Ipswich (for FN*)	

Trafford Park.

DRS built on the success of its Anglo-Scottish operation and introduced several new services in 2004/05. The first was a seven-days-a-week service for the Malcolm Group between Grangemouth and Aberdeen, using a new railhead at Aberdeen Craiginches. This was followed by a weekdays-only service between Grangemouth and Elderslie, covering a distance of just 35

Birmingham Landor Street Freightliner terminal remained busy in the early years of the 21st century despite competition from independent railheads at Hams Hall and Birch Coppice. No 66502 awaits departure from Landor Street with 4L90, the 1408 to Ipswich, on 31 October 2003.

miles and providing a useful alternative to the heavily congested A80 road. In May 2005 DRS inaugurated a train between Widnes and Purfleet in partnership with terminal operator AHC Warehousing and logistics provider Novatrans, connecting with the Cobelfret crossing to Zeebrugge.

EWS pursued the trend towards trainload operation. In late 2004 it shed most of its less-than-trainload intermodal traffic, including some small-scale flows to and from Purfleet and Tilbury. In 2005 it began a new trainload service between Hams Hall and Tilbury, specifically designed for 9ft 6in containers and

Freightliner timetable, January 2004 (Continued)					
4L75	1014	MSX	Trafford Park	Ipswich (for FN*)	
4O29	1314	SO	Trafford Park	Southampton MCT	
4O29	1414	SX	Trafford Park	Southampton MCT	
4O08	1914	SX	Trafford Park	Southampton MCT	
4O80	2139	SX	Trafford Park	Thamesport	
4L82	2316	SX	Trafford Park	Ipswich (for FN*)	
4L56	0230	MX	Wentloog	Ipswich (for FN*)	
4O51	1008	SX	Wentloog	Millbrook	
4M68	2332	SX	Wentloog	Crewe Basford Hall	
4D07	1428	SX	Wilton	Leeds	
4L79	1610	SX	Wilton	Felixstowe North	

* FS = Felixstowe South, FN = Felixstowe North

Felixstowe strengthened its position as the number one port for UK intermodal traffic. By the end of 2005 Freightliner alone was running

connecting with Geest North Sea Line ferries to Rotterdam and Bilbao. Later in the year EWS started a short-distance Thamesport to Willesden service for Containerlift; however, the economics of that operation were poor and it lasted only a few months.

Birch Coppice intermodal terminal opened in 2006, taking a share of the buoyant deep-sea intermodal traffic to and from the West Midlands. For a time it handled regular services for three operators: Freightliner, EWS and Fastline. No 66570 pulls out of the terminal with 4O97, the 1800 Freightliner departure to Southampton Maritime, on 22 August 2006.

Intermodal terminals, 2005			
Terminal	Operator(s)	Terminal	Operator(s)
Aberdeen	DRS	Hams Hall	EWS, Freightliner, GB Railfreight
Grangemouth	DRS, EWS	Birmingham Landor Street	Freightliner
Coatbridge	Freightliner	Daventry	EWS, DRS, Freightliner
Mossend EWS	EWS	Ely	EWS
Mossend Russells	DRS	Willesden	EWS
Elderslie	DRS	Barking Ripple Lane	Freightliner
Wilton	Freightliner	Purfleet	EWS*, DRS
Tees Dock	EWS	Tilbury Freightliner	Freightliner
Selby	GB Railfreight	Tilbury Riverside	EWS*
Leeds	Freightliner	Felixstowe South	Freightliner, EWS, GB Railfreight
Wakefield	EWS	Felixstowe North	Freightliner
Doncaster	EWS*	Thamesport	Freightliner, EWS
Immingham	EWS*	Avonmouth	EWS*
Trafford Park	Freightliner	Cardiff Wentloog	Freightliner, EWS*
Barton Dock	Freightliner	Barry	EWS*
Trafford Park	EWS	Southampton Millbrook	Freightliner
Widnes O'Connors	Freightliner	Southampton Maritime	Freightliner
Widnes AHC	EWS, DRS	Southampton Western Docks	EWS
Garston	Freightliner		
Seaforth	Freightliner	*served by wagonload network	
Burton-on-Trent	EWS, GB Railfreight		

Fastline made a promising entry to the intermodal market and achieved reasonable loadings for a time on its trains from Doncaster and Birch Coppice to Thamesport. No 56302, one of three Class 56 locomotives returned to service with Fastline, passes Ryecroft Junction with 4O90, the 1101 Doncaster to Thamesport train, on 14 February 2007.

RAILFREIGHT: CONTAINERS, CARS AND SPECIAL TRAFFICS

Victa Railfreight took over the operation of Tilbury Riverside freight terminal in 2002. The terminal handled a daily Freightliner train from Felixstowe and, until March 2002, a Freightliner service from Leeds. The Felixstowe train included a short-term flow of contaminated soil and ballast from a rail-locked track renewal site at Ipswich yard, carried in bags on a single intermodal wagon. RFS-owned locomotive No 08764 shunts a train including one of the Ipswich wagons at Tilbury Riverside on 22 October 2002.

Daventry was one of the most successful terminals set up to handle Channel Tunnel intermodal traffic, although increasingly it was geared to handling deep-sea and domestic flows. Its location on the West Coast Main Line was a major factor in its success. By 2006 it was handling some 80,000 containers a year and had a schedule of 126 trains a week. Pilot locomotive No 08844 shunts a trainload of deep-sea boxes for Felixstowe at Daventry on 22 August 2006.

Direct Rail Services made a striking impact with its Stobart Rail/Tesco trains between Daventry and Grangemouth, even though the 'Less CO_2' slogan clashed somewhat with the use of diesel traction under the wires. No 66411 *Eddie the Engine* passes Hardrigg with 4S43, the 0631 Daventry to Grangemouth 'Tesco Express' train, on 6 June 2007.

19 trains a day from the port, serving a total of 13 destinations, which now included Daventry and Doncaster. Three further departures from Felixstowe were operated by GBRf, and two by EWS. A fourth GBRf train, serving Doncaster, would be introduced in early 2006. To cater for continued growth the Hutchison Ports Holding Group authorised expenditure of up to £50 million to double-track a 4½-mile stretch of the Felixstowe branch.

During 2005 Freightliner invested heavily in its wagon fleet. Having already ordered 80 additional FLA low-deck wagons in 2003, it now placed an order for 166 FEA standard-height wagons, which would enable the withdrawal of the surviving 1960s-vintage FFA/FGAs and some of its hired KFAs. Freightliner also continued to renew its locomotive fleet, with 33 Class 66s allocated to the intermodal business by the end of 2006 and more on the way. The 12 Freightliner Class 57s were gradually relegated to lighter duties and would be phased out completely between May 2007 and April 2008.

DB Schenker took over haulage of the 'Tesco Express' as part of its contract with Stobart Rail in early 2010. No 92017 approaches Docker on 4 January with the first working of 4S43, the 0625 from Rugby to Mossend. The use of Rugby instead of Daventry at the southern end of the route was an unexpected move.

Fastline Freight entered the intermodal market in 2006, having acquired 24 FEA wagons and the use of three reinstated Class 56 locomotives. It ran a daily train from Thamesport to either Birch Coppice or Doncaster Railport. Birch Coppice was a new container terminal, located at the end of the former colliery branch that had reopened in 2002 for Volkswagen component traffic. By late 2006 Birch Coppice was also handling two daily trains to and from Southampton, one operated by EWS and the other by Freightliner, in addition to the Fastline business.

Another new intermodal operator was FM Rail, which teamed up with Victa Railfreight to run a Hams Hall to Mossend service from November 2006, using double Class 47 haulage. However, that service was cut short by the collapse of FM Rail. Victa Railfreight then joined forces with Westlink, part of the Stobart Group, to form Victa Westlink, which offered an intermodal service linking Tilbury, Purfleet, Widnes and Grangemouth. That service initially used KAA 'Mega 3' wagons that had been built for the short-lived 'Piggyback' operation for Lafarge cement, later switching to IKA 'Megafrets'. It ran until the autumn of 2007.

DRS's strong presence on the Anglo-Scottish corridor was boosted in 2006 when it signed a three-year deal with haulier Eddie Stobart and

Direct Services gained a foothold on North Thamesside by extending its intermodal operations from Daventry to Ripple Lane and Tilbury. No 66414 *James the Engine* departs from the former Freightliner terminal at Ripple Lane with 4M71, the 1248 intermodal train to Daventry, on 27 August 2009.

EWS acquired regular intermodal traffic to and from Barry, which fed into the Enterprise network at Newport Alexandra Dock Junction yard. The destinations for the boxes included Southampton, Tilbury and Immingham. Yard pilot No 09013 shunts FKA wagons from Barry at Alexandra Dock Junction on 6 June 2006, ready to join the 6M17 Enterprise service to Wembley.

retailer Tesco for a daily service between Daventry and Grangemouth. Each train would consist of 13 IKA 'Megafret' twin-set wagons and would convey 26 8-foot curtain-sided containers with Stobart Rail/Tesco branding. The deal was supported by various grants, including a £200,000 Freight Facilities Grant for Eddie Stobart to buy 90 containers and a £235,000 Company Neutral Revenue Support payment from the Department for Transport. The decision to use 8-foot containers was

taken in order to ensure that, when the West Coast Main Line was unavailable, the train could easily be diverted over routes with a more restrictive loading gauge. Press releases issued at the time stressed the environmental benefits of the Tesco traffic switching to rail – the loss of 4½ million lorry journeys would save 6,000 tonnes of CO_2 emissions from being pumped into the atmosphere – even though DRS would be using Class 66 diesel traction under the wires for most of the journey.

Intermodal losses in 2006 included the DRS Widnes to Purfleet service, which had struggled to attract business, and EWS trains from Felixstowe and Southampton to Ely. In place of the Ely trains came new services from Felixstowe and Southampton to Trafford Park. EWS withdrew one of its two daily trains on the Daventry to Mossend route as a result of the loss of Russells traffic to DRS. Freightliner withdrew its Southampton to Wilton service following the diversion of some former P&O Nedlloyd (now Maersk) business from Southampton to Felixstowe. That move left Wilton with just one daily train, serving Felixstowe. In January 2007 the already under-utilised Wentloog terminal saw its Freightliner service reduced to a single route to and from Southampton, Freightliner having decided that the connecting train to Crewe for Felixstowe traffic was no longer viable. Another

loss in 2007 was the former P&O Nedlloyd train from Southampton to Ripple Lane, leaving Freightliner with no regular business at its Ripple Lane terminal.

The year 2008 began with high hopes for Scottish intermodal traffic as a £4 million gauge enhancement scheme was completed, allowing 8ft 6in containers to be carried on standard wagons to Aberdeen and Elgin. EWS introduced a weekly service between Grangemouth and Elgin, but ironically this train was routed via the Highland main line to share haulage with the oil tanks to Lairg. The service was soon withdrawn due to poor loadings. A more successful addition to the Scottish intermodal timetable was a DRS-operated train from Grangemouth to Inverness for Stobart, launched in November 2008. DRS had also expanded its territory south of the border, with a new service from Tilbury and Ripple Lane to Daventry running twice weekly from June and later increasing to five trains a week.

The economic recession took its toll on some intermodal flows in 2009. Fastline pulled out of intermodal traffic altogether, putting an end to its Thamesport-based services, which had briefly included Trafford Park as well as Doncaster and Birch Coppice. Freightliner had withdrawn its link to the Port of Liverpool terminal at Seaforth in September 2008, leaving just one weekly EWS-hauled steel train using that facility. During 2009 Freightliner mothballed its Millbrook terminal at Southampton, as its main Maritime terminal could handle

The first Class 66 locomotive to receive DB Schenker colours was No 66152, outshopped from Toton in January 2009. Only three other locomotives received the new livery during 2009 – Nos 59206, 37419 and 37670. No 66152 passes Oakenshaw with 4L28, the 1410 Wakefield to Tilbury empty container train, on 18 March 2009.

It took a very long time for the Donnington branch to be reopened and, when it finally happened, rail traffic to the new intermodal terminal amounted to less than one train a week, carrying traffic for the adjacent military depot. No 66143 waits at Donnington on 17 December 2009, having arrived on 6G51, the 0751 departure from Warrington Arpley.

all the traffic then on offer. A new intermodal terminal at Fratton, serving Portsmouth, opened at the end of 2008 and was used by a twice-weekly EWS (later DBS) service, but it failed to generate enough traffic and was mothballed within weeks. EWS gave up two of its Tilbury flows, one carrying fruit to Wakefield and the other general traffic to Wentloog, reducing the EWS presence at Tilbury to occasional wagonload consignments from Barry. The long-awaited Donnington terminal handled its first, DRS-hauled, test train in February 2009 but struggled to find regular intermodal business, the only revenue-earning business during that year turning out to be an occasional DBS-hauled feeder service from Warrington for the Ministry of Defence.

Against that gloomy background, there were some 'green shoots'. Birch Coppice intermodal terminal continued to thrive and attracted three new services in the space of three weeks in the summer of 2009: DBS provided a service from Thamesport, First GBRf from Felixstowe and Freightliner from Southampton. In September 2009 DBS launched a Hams Hall to Mossend service, sharing traction with an existing Trafford Park to Mossend train from Crewe, while in the same month DRS started a second train on

the Highland main line, carrying boxes for Russells between Coatbridge and Inverness. Meanwhile Stobart Rail announced that it was moving its rail operations from DRS to DBS from January 2010. This would mean DBS taking over the existing Stobart Rail services between Daventry, Central Scotland and Inverness, as well as potentially extending the network to other regions. However, DBS introduced cost-cutting measures in early 2010, which resulted in the mothballing of its Trafford Park and Grangemouth terminals, with some traffic lost to road and other flows diverted to Mossend and Wakefield respectively.

Looking to the longer term, two major loading gauge enhancement projects were announced in 2009, which ought at least to enable rail to retain its market share of deep-sea traffic from key ports despite the rising proportion of 9ft 6in boxes. The first was the £71 million enhancement of the Southampton to Nuneaton corridor to W10 gauge, including major works in Southampton Tunnel, which was expected to be completed by 2011. The second project, announced in December 2009, was a £42.5 million upgrade of the cross-country route between Felixstowe and Nuneaton to W10 gauge, providing a useful alternative to the increasingly congested lines through London. The Felixstowe upgrade would include a new curve at Ipswich to cut out the need to run round in Ipswich yard.

Several 9ft 6in containers stand out prominently as two container trains meet at Hademore on 29 May 2009. Heading north is No 90048 with 4M87, the 1143 Freightliner service from Felixstowe to Trafford Park, while the up slow line is occupied by a Felixstowe-bound train.

The loading gauge problem

Compared with many overseas railways, Britain's rail system suffers from restrictive loading gauges on many routes, making it difficult to cater for the growing number of 9ft 6in 'high cube' deep-sea containers. While the best solution for the freight operator is to increase clearances on the railway, that takes a lot of money and time and operators have therefore had to invest in low-deck rolling-stock.

Freightliner introduced two types of wagon that can carry 9ft 6in on routes with a W8 or W9 gauge restriction: small-wheeled low-deck bogie container flats coded FLA, and Finnish-built 'pocket' wagons coded KTA (originally KQA). The main advantage of the KTAs over the FLAs is that they have standard-size wheels, enabling an axle loading of 22.5 tonnes rather than just 13 tonnes for an FLA. On the other hand the KTAs have a usable deck length of just 40 feet for a total buffer-to-buffer wagon length of 68 feet, meaning that fewer containers can be carried for a given length of train.

DB Schenker catered for 'high cube' boxes on restricted routes in a similar way to Freightliner, with a mixture of FKA flat-deck wagons and FAA well wagons. Both DB Schenker and Direct Rail Services used low-deck IKA 'Megafrets'.

Maximum container heights for intermodal wagons on W8 and W9 routes, December 2009			
Wagon	Operator	W8 gauge	W9 gauge
FLA	Freightliner 'lowliner'	9ft 6in	9ft 6in
KTA	GE Rail Services 'pocket'	9ft 6in	9ft 6in
FAA	DBS well wagon	9ft 0in	9ft 6in
FKA	DBS	9ft 0in	9ft 6in
IKA	'Megafret'	9ft 0in	9ft 6in
FIA	DBS	8ft 6in	9ft 0in
FSA	Freightliner	8ft 6in	9ft 0in
FTA	Freightliner	8ft 6in	9ft 0in
IFA	'Multifret'	8ft 6in	9ft 0in
FEA	Freightliner/First GBRf	8ft 6in	8ft 9in
KFA	Tiphook	8ft 6in	8ft 9in
FCA	DBS	8ft 0in	8ft 6in

2.
Channel Tunnel Intermodal

When in July 1987 the Channel Tunnel Act gained Royal Assent, it was widely assumed that cross-Channel rail freight traffic faced a rosy future. The existence of a fixed link would reduce dramatically the journey time for Anglo-European flows compared with the cumbersome train ferry. As tunnel construction got under way, so BR and its French partner SNCF developed plans to make the most of the opportunity. In 1993, one year ahead of the tunnel's opening, BR's distribution arm, Railfreight Distribution (RfD), negotiated an initial total of 11 daily paths in each direction between Wembley and the French terminal at Fréthun. The requirement was expected to rise to 35 paths by 1997, carrying a gross volume of six million tonnes a year. Most of the business would be intermodal, with regular services likely to serve seven terminals in the UK and 20 in mainland Europe.

The infrastructure for Channel Tunnel rail freight on the British side of the water included Dollands Moor sidings near the tunnel portal and Wembley European Freight Operating Centre a few miles north of central London. The facilities at Dollands Moor were limited to six holding sidings, of which four were allocated to export traffic and two to import traffic. Except in emergencies no wagons were to be shunted at Dollands Moor: its purpose was to hold trains awaiting a change of locomotive and/or crew or while awaiting a path on the main line. Wembley was a much bigger affair, with 29 sidings, 10 miles of track and 70 sets of points. Wembley would act as the portion exchange point for less-than-trainload flows via the tunnel, including conventional wagon and automotive traffic as well as intermodal business.

The seven designated locations for loading and unloading Channel Tunnel intermodal traffic in the UK included three existing Freightliner terminals at Birmingham Landor Street, Wilton, Cardiff Pengam and Liverpool Seaforth, and new purpose-built Euroterminals at Willesden, Mossend and Trafford Park. An additional

Dollands Moor provided limited siding accommodation for trains awaiting their path through the Channel Tunnel or to London, as well as for changes of locomotive and crew. Nos 92010 and 92012 stand at Dollands Moor with train 44404 to Fréthun on 31 May 2001, while No 92043 waits on the adjacent track.

Trafford Park was one of the first Channel Tunnel intermodal terminals to be completed. It was located near the existing Freightliner terminal, but with independent rail and road access. The completed facility is pictured on 7 October 1993, still awaiting its first business but temporarily playing host to Railfreight Distribution's 'European collection' of Class 90 locomotives, variously painted in French, Belgian and German liveries. Once it became clear that the potential for Channel Tunnel business was limited, Trafford Park began to handle EWS domestic and deep-sea intermodal traffic, with flows to and from Grangemouth, Tees Dock, Southampton and Felixstowe. The last Channel Tunnel traffic at Trafford Park ceased in 2009 and the terminal closed completely in 2010.

Euroterminal at Wakefield would come on stream later. In 1993 RfD produced a provisional timetable for intermodal services between these terminals and 13 locations in mainland Europe, with journey times ranging from 13 hours for Willesden to Muizen in Belgium to 54 hours for Mossend to Avignon.

The traction for Channel Tunnel intermodal traffic on electrified routes would be taken from the pool of 46 Class 92 locomotives, of which 37 would be owned by BR and nine by SNCF. The dual-voltage capability of the Class 92s meant that they could operate on the 750V DC third rail system in Kent as well as on 25kV AC through the tunnel and on the West and East Coast Main Lines. Once it was clear that delivery of the Class 92s was delayed, arrangements were put in place for the temporary use of SNCF 22200 Class electrics through the tunnel, giving way to diesels at Dollands Moor.

The intermodal wagon fleet would consist of 450 'Multifret' twin sets, of which half would be owned by RfD and coded FIA and the remainder split between SNCF and Intercontainer and coded IFA. With their deck height of 945mm, the 'Multifrets' could carry boxes up to 9 feet high and 8ft 2½in wide on the core routes from Dollands Moor to Wembley (via Maidstone and via Redhill), Wembley to Birmingham, Liverpool, Manchester and Mossend, and Wembley to Leeds and Newcastle. Each twin set could carry up to two 40-foot-long boxes or four 20-foot-long boxes. An increasing proportion of the boxes conveyed through the tunnel was expected to be non-stackable swapbodies, rather than deep-sea-type ISO containers.

While RfD would be the UK rail haulier for all Channel Tunnel traffic, it would act only as a wholesaler as far as selling space on its trains was concerned. The marketing and retailing of

Channel Tunnel intermodal timetable, March 1995					
Code	Dep	Days	From	To	Also detaches or attaches traffic at
4A36	1405	SX	Birmingham	Wembley	
4A25	2148	SX	Birmingham	Wembley	
*7M05	1901	SX	Dagenham Dock	Wembley	
4M72	1026	SX	Mossend	Wembley	
4M74	1442	SX	Mossend	Wembley	
4M84	1825	SX	Mossend	Wembley	
4A02	1850	SX	Seaforth	Wembley	
4A13	1310	SX	Trafford Park	Wembley	
4A14	2152	SX	Trafford Park	Wembley	
4A20	0148	MX	Willesden	Wembley	
4A83	0805	MFX	Willesden	Wembley	
4A87	1802	SX	Willesden	Wembley	
4A79	2105	SX	Willesden	Wembley	
4A91	2338	SX	Willesden	Wembley	
4O48	0123	WThFO	Wembley	Dollands Moor	
4O49	0210	MX	Wembley	Dollands Moor	
4O52	0322	MX	Wembley	Dollands Moor	
4O53	0333	MX	Wembley	Dollands Moor	
4O56	0937	MFX	Wembley	Dollands Moor	
4O63	1218	SX	Wembley	Dollands Moor	Willesden
4O70	1920	SX	Wembley	Dollands Moor	Willesden
4O71	2008	SX	Wembley	Dollands Moor	
*7O72	2037	SX	Wembley	Dollands Moor	
4O78	2250	SX	Wembley	Dollands Moor	
4M14	0212	MSX	Dollands Moor	Wembley	Willesden
4M15	0222	MTX	Dollands Moor	Wembley	
4M16	0312	MX	Dollands Moor	Wembley	Willesden
7M17	0317	MX	Dollands Moor	Wembley	
4M29	1114	SuO	Dollands Moor	Wembley	
4M31	1215	SO	Dollands Moor	Wembley	
4M31	1215	WThFO	Dollands Moor	Wembley	Willesden
4M32	1314	SuO	Dollands Moor	Wembley	
4M33	1414	SuO	Dollands Moor	Wembley	
4M36	1742	MX	Dollands Moor	Wembley	
4M38	1850	TWThO	Dollands Moor	Wembley	
*7M39	1910	SuO	Dollands Moor	Wembley	

intermodal services was entrusted to specialist companies such as Combined Transport Limited (CTL), Allied Continental Intermodal (ACI) and Unilog, replicating the structures already in place in mainland Europe. These companies would book space on RfD trains and would charter their own trains as soon as business built up sufficiently on a given route.

The first intermodal train through the Channel Tunnel, a Unilog service from Muizen to Willesden, ran on 2 June 1994. Other trains were soon added to the timetable. By March 1995 RfD was running trains for CTL, ACI and Unilog between UK terminals at Willesden, Birmingham Landor Street, Trafford Park, Seaforth and Mossend, and mainland European terminals at Muizen, Duisburg, Paris (Valenton and Noisy), Lyon, Avignon, Perpignan, Milano (Rogoredo and Smistamento), Melzo and Novara. The planned Channel Tunnel terminal at Wakefield was not yet complete and neither Wilton nor Cardiff Pengam was served. Because there was not enough business for block trains, portions between different pairs of destinations were split and recombined at Wembley. This resulted in a complex train plan, as shown in the accompanying table. Class 92 locomotives started hauling trains through the tunnel in February 1995, but it would be a long time before their full network capability was achieved.

Some of the European locations were interchange points for destinations further afield. The ACI hub at Paris Valenton,

Channel Tunnel intermodal timetable, March 1995					
Code	Dep	Days	From	To	Also detaches or attaches traffic at
4M42	2014	SuO	Dollands Moor	Wembley	
4M52	2115	MSX	Dollands Moor	Wembley	Willesden
4M52	2115	SO	Dollands Moor	Wembley	
4M55	2142	WThFO	Dollands Moor	Wembley	Willesden
4M63	2315	MX	Dollands Moor	Wembley	
4G13	0328	TX	Wembley	Birmingham	
4G15	0601	MX	Wembley	Birmingham	
*7L23	0604	SO	Wembley	Dagenham Dock	
*7L23	0608	SX	Wembley	Dagenham Dock	
4S90	0318	MTX	Wembley	Mossend	
4S90	0346	MO	Wembley	Mossend	
4S73	0545	MX	Wembley	Mossend	
4F01	0219	MO	Wembley	Seaforth	
4F01	0223	MTX	Wembley	Seaforth	
4H06	0152	MO	Wembley	Trafford Park	
4H05	0252	MTX	Wembley	Trafford Park	
4H34	0620	SO	Wembley	Trafford Park	
4H34	0630	MSX	Wembley	Trafford Park	
4A88	0128	MO	Wembley	Willesden	
4A74	0239	TX	Wembley	Willesden	
4A82	0559	MTX	Wembley	Willesden	
4A96	2255	MSX	Wembley	Willesden	
* automotive components					

The first addition to the UK Channel Tunnel intermodal network was Wakefield, which opened in January 1996. However, traffic from Wakefield was slow to develop, largely because it was too close to Trafford Park. Another terminal that struggled to get established was Seaforth, which lost its RfD service in September 1996 in favour of tagging any Channel Tunnel intermodal wagons on to the back of a Freightliner train. However, the relatively short-distance Unilog operation linking Muizen with Willesden and Trafford Park outstripped its capacity and a second daily train was introduced on this route in September 1997.

The year 1997 saw the opening of two Channel Tunnel intermodal terminals in the West Midlands, replacing the shared use of the Freightliner facility at Birmingham Landor Street. The first was Daventry, which opened in May for services to and from Milano. The second was Hams Hall, opened in July. Both Daventry and Hams Hall were independently run terminals that embraced the 'freight village' concept promoted by BR and Channel Tunnel operators, with ample space for warehousing at the site. Daventry had the advantage of being located on the electrified West Coast Main Line, enabling trains between London and the North West to call there en route.

The success of the Transfesa automotive component trains between Ford plants at Silla and Dagenham led Forth Ports to set up a distribution railhead at Tilbury, where Transfesa could backload the Ford swapbodies with general freight from the UK to Spain. The 5¼-acre railhead was built on the site of Tilbury Riverside passenger station and was given the title Tilbury International Freight Terminal. Unfortunately it did not generate enough business to justify its use

for example, offered connections to 28 further locations in France. Milano was a hub for five further locations in Italy. Muizen offered a connection to Morocco via Cadiz and Tangier. Duisburg was the base for connections to Berlin, Bremen, Frankfurt, München and Nürnberg. The list of traffic types conveyed by Channel Tunnel freight services was vast and included, to name but a few, bulk orange juice, bulk wine, packaged wine, detergents, crisps, clothing, footwear, paper, steel coil, steel pipes, fabricated steelwork, electronic goods, electrical appliances, knock-down furniture, ceramics, tiles and cat litter.

by the Transfesa trains, which reverted to carrying Ford import traffic only.

On 22 November 1997 all Channel Tunnel intermodal traffic officially passed to EWS as part of its purchase of RfD. This merger gave EWS the flexibility to use Channel Tunnel intermodal terminals and Class 92 locomotives on domestic as well as Channel Tunnel traffic, although the Class 92s were still severely restricted in their operations and at one point EWS considered not taking them. Channel Tunnel intermodal business grew under EWS management, but

The low traffic volume through the tunnel forced EWS to rethink the original plans to run block trains directly between a single terminal in Britain and a single terminal in mainland Europe. Instead, most trains were re-formed at Wembley yard, with feeder services operating between Wembley and the various terminals. No 92023 *Ravel* waits to depart from Wembley with containers bound for Melzo in northern Italy on the evening of 22 July 1999.

Channel Tunnel intermodal terminals and services, 1998		
Terminal	Operator	Number of services in each direction per week (approx.)
UK		
Willesden	EWS International	23
Tilbury	Transfesa	-
Daventry	Tibbet & Britten	13
Hams Hall	Parsec	11
Trafford Park	EWS International	22
Liverpool Seaforth	Liverpool Freeport	5 (Freightliner connection)
Wakefield	EWS International	6
Mossend	EWS International	10
Mainland Europe		
Muizen	Unilog	10
Metz	ICF	5
Paris Valenton	CTI, CNC	8
Lyon/Avignon/Perpignan	ACI	4
Torino	ACI, CTI	5
Novara	CTI	6
Oleggio	ACI	5
Milano Segrate/Rogoredo	ACI, CTI	12

Right **Hams Hall took over from Birmingham Landor Street as the Channel Tunnel intermodal railhead for the West Midlands in 1997. Nos 47360 and 47298 join the main line at Whitacre Junction with 4A36, the 1418 Hams Hall to Wembley train, on 4 April 1998. At that time Class 47 locomotives were commonly rostered in pairs as a breakdown precaution.**

Below **Belgian-liveried locomotive No 90128 *Vrachtverbinding* passes Winwick Junction with 4M72, the 1020 Mossend to Wembley Channel Tunnel intermodal train, on 15 February 1997. At that time the timetable showed two daily Channel Tunnel intermodal departures from Mossend, but in practice only one was a regular runner.**

Channel Tunnel rail freight: gross volume, million tonnes	
1995	1.35
1996	2.78
1997	2.93
1998	3.14
1999	2.87
2000	2.95
2001	2.45
2002	1.46
2003	1.74
2004	1.89
2005	1.58
2006	1.57
2007	1.21
2008	1.24
2009	1.18

only slowly: in 1998 the total rail freight carryings via the tunnel reached 3.1 million tonnes, still far short of the 6 million tonnes that had originally been predicted. The most fertile ground in Europe for Channel Tunnel intermodal traffic was northern Italy, accounting for more than half of the scheduled trains.

As things turned out, Channel Tunnel rail freight failed to rise above its 1998 level. Issues of service reliability undermined the confidence of customers, who were already paying a premium to use rail rather than road. The total throughput declined to just under 2.9 million tonnes in 1999 and was only slightly higher than that in 2000. There were a few gains during that time, notably the starting up of a direct intermodal service between Bari and Trafford Park, catering mainly for imports of Italian furniture, but the established flows to and from France,

Belgium and northern Italy were at best stable.

In 2001 EWS and the freight division of SNCF launched a joint initiative called Channel Rail Freight in an attempt to improve the quality of service and attract more customers to the tunnel. Channel Rail Freight enabled customers to buy end-to-end transits, generally at 24 hours notice, from a single combined marketing team, based in London but comprising both SNCF and EWS staff. The second purpose of Channel Rail Freight was to improve customer service by tracking the progress of Channel Tunnel wagons throughout their journey and informing customers of any delays or other problems. Delays were all too commonplace: between 1998 and

2000 the proportion of Italian services arriving within 60 minutes of their booked time had fallen from 75% to 62%.

In an effort to reduce costs and improve service reliability, Channel Rail Freight restructured the timetable for intermodal services by reducing the role of Wembley yard and running most trains as a block unit between one terminal in the UK and one terminal in mainland Europe, much as had originally been planned back in the late 1980s. An inevitable result of this change was to reduce the number of journey permutations. Hams Hall, for example, retained direct services only to and from Milano, whereas previously it had handled traffic to and

Channel Tunnel rail freight, June 2001

Scheduled departures from Dollands Moor – import traffic

Code	Days	From	Dep D Moor	To	Traffic	Company
4M00	TThFSO	Milano Rogoredo	0005	Hams Hall	Intermodal	ACI
6B02	MX	Publier/Riom	0025	Wembley	Trainload	
4M06	MO	Metz	0105	Daventry	Intermodal	ACI
4M06	MX	Paris Valenton	0113	Daventry	Intermodal	CNC
6B08	WThFO	Somain	0140	Wembley	Enterprise	
4M14	MX	Muizen	0256	Trafford Park	Intermodal	Unilog
6V95	MO	Alessandria	0300	Exeter Riverside	Trainload	
4M18	TThO	Paris Noisy	0317	Trafford Park	Intermodal	CTL
4B18	SO	Paris Noisy	0317	Wembley	Intermodal	CTL
7L23	MSX	Almussafes	0417	Dagenham	Intermodal	Transfesa
7L20	SO	Almussafes	0417	Dagenham	Intermodal	Transfesa
4M23	TFO	Paris Valenton	0845	Daventry	Intermodal	CNC
4B24	SuO	Milano Rogoredo	0914	Wembley	Intermodal	ACI
6M24	MTX	Lonato	0920	Washwood Heath	Automotive	
4B26	SuO	Paris Valenton	1014	Wembley	Intermodal	CNC
6M26	SO	Achères	1018	Corby	Automotive	
6M26	MSX	Achères	1020	Corby	Automotive	
6M28	TThO	Creutzwald	1043	Washwood Heath	Automotive	
4B28	SuO	Muizen	1114	Wembley	Intermodal	Unilog
6M28	SO	Creutzwald	1121	Washwood Heath	Automotive	

Channel Tunnel rail freight, June 2001 (Continued)						
6B34	TThO	Publier/Riom	1145	Wembley	Trainload	
6M90	SuO	Lonato	1200	Washwood Heath	Automotive	
4M76	TThFO	Bari	1220	Trafford Park	Intermodal	GTS
7B32	SuO	Almussafes	1314	Wembley	Intermodal	Transfesa
6B32	WThFO	Somain	1342	Wembley	Enterprise	
6B34	SO	Somain	1342	Wembley	Enterprise	
6B38	SuO	Somain	1614	Wembley	Enterprise	
6M42	TThO	Santa Vittoria	1719	Daventry	Trainload	
6B38	SO	Santa Vittoria	1740	Wembley	Trainload	
6B46	SX	Zeebrugge	1845	Wembley	Trainload	
6B46	SuO	Zeebrugge	1914	Wembley	Trainload	
4M48	WThFO	Novara	1915	Daventry	Intermodal	CTL
4B48	SO	Novara	1915	Wembley	Intermodal	CTL
6B66	MO	Lille La Délivrance	1950	Wembley	Enterprise	
4M50	SuO	Novara	2014	Daventry	Intermodal	CTL
4B50	WFSO	Melzo	2015	Wembley	Intermodal	CTL
4B52	SuO	Melzo	2114	Wembley	Intermodal	CTL
4B56	TWFO	Milano Rogoredo	2120	Willesden	Intermodal	CTL
4B56	SO	Milano Rogoredo	2148	Wembley	Intermodal	CTL
6B56	MO	Sibelin	2205	Wembley	Enterprise	
4B56	SuO	Milano Rogoredo	2214	Willesden	Intermodal	CTL
6M59	MO	Carimate	2235	Washwood Heath	Automotive	
6M60	SX	Köln Gremberg	2242	Bescot	Enterprise	
6B60	SO	Köln Gremberg	2247	Wembley	Enterprise	
4M62	WThFO	Milano Smistamento	2315	Hams Hall	Intermodal	ACI
4B62	SO	Milano Smistamento	2315	Wembley	Intermodal	ACI
6B64	SuO	Publier/Riom	2345	Wembley	Trainload	
4M64	WThO	Metz	2345	Daventry	Intermodal	ACI

from five or six European locations using feeders to and from Wembley. Seaforth finally lost its Channel Tunnel intermodal service altogether and Mossend was cut to just two Channel Tunnel intermodal departures a week. In mainland Europe the often poorly loaded train to Avignon and Perpignan was withdrawn.

While Channel Rail Freight put useful measures in place to improve customer service, there was one problem over which it had only limited control: security. Increasing numbers of illegal immigrants were smuggling themselves into containers and EWS was fined for each immigrant discovered on one of its trains. By mid-2001 those fines had amounted to more than £600,000. Unfortunately things only got worse. In November 2001 waves of asylum-seekers invaded the yard at Fréthun and forced SNCF to reduce drastically the number of freight trains using the tunnel. For six months EWS could only run 40% of normal services, not only causing the company to lose £10 million in potential revenue

Channel Tunnel rail freight, June 2001

Scheduled arrivals at Dollands Moor – export traffic

Code	Days	From	To	Arr D Moor	Traffic	Company
6O64	ThSX	Bordesley	Lonato	0016	Automotive	
6O69	SX	Corby	Achères	0042	Automotive	
6B05	MSX	Wembley	Köln Gremberg	0301	Enterprise	
4B03	WThFO	Wembley	Melzo	0308	Intermodal	CTL
4O83	WO	Mossend	Paris Valenton	0317	Intermodal	CTL
4O07	TThFO	Daventry	Metz	0356	Intermodal	ACI
4O09	TThFO	Hams Hall	Milano Rogoredo	0416	Intermodal	ACI
4B13	MTX	Willesden	Milano Rogoredo	0513	Intermodal	CTL
6B19	TThO	Wembley	Lille La Délivrance	0555	Enterprise	
4O21	WThFO	Daventry	Novara	0622	Intermodal	CTL
4O23	WThO	Hams Hall	Milano Smistamento	0658	Intermodal	ACI
4O23	SO	Hams Hall	Milano Smistamento	0702	Intermodal	ACI
6B25	MX	Wembley	Lille La Délivrance	0818	Enterprise	
4O33	SO	Trafford Park	Bari	1116	Intermodal	GTS
6B35	SuO	Wembley	Zeebrugge	1144	Trainload	
4O33	WFO	Trafford Park	Bari	1152	Intermodal	GTS
6B37	SX	Wembley	Lille La Délivrance	1214	Enterprise	
6B37	SO	Wembley	Lille La Délivrance	1219	Enterprise	
4B41	SuO	Wembley	Paris Valenton	1229	Intermodal	CNC
6O41	MWFO	Corby	Creutzwald	1424	Automotive	
4B45	SuO	Wembley	Milano Smistamento	1429	Intermodal	ACI
6O45	SX	Barking	Zeebrugge	1447	Trainload	
7B49	SuO	Wembley	Silla	1546	Intermodal	Transfesa
4B53	SuO	Wembley	Paris Noisy	1644	Intermodal	CTL
6O92	MO	Exeter Riverside	Alessandria	1755	Trainload	
4O63	WO	Tyne Dock	Carimate	1803	Automotive	
6O55	SuO	Washwood Heath	Lonato	1820	Automotive	
4B57	SuO	Wembley	Paris Valenton	1844	Intermodal	CNC
4O59	SO	Daventry	Novara	1848	Intermodal	CTL
4O61	SO	Hams Hall	Milano Rogoredo	1947	Intermodal	ACI
4O63	SO	Daventry	Muizen	2051	Intermodal	Unilog

Channel Tunnel rail freight, June 2001 (Continued)						
4O94	SX	Daventry	Paris Valenton	2141	Intermodal	CNC
4O69	SX	Trafford Park	Muizen	2146	Intermodal	Unilog
4O71	TThO	Trafford Park	Paris Noisy	2216	Intermodal	CTL
4O73	SO	Trafford Park	Milano Rogoredo	2253	Intermodal	CTL
7Z81	SX	Dagenham	Silla	2326	Intermodal	Transfesa
4B67	SO	Wembley	Melzo	2335	Intermodal	CTL
6O79	MWFO	Daventry	Santa Vittoria	2351	Trainload	UDV

but also undermining the fragile confidence of its customers. Eventually the security at Fréthun was improved and normal services could resume, but not before many customers had made alternative arrangements for their business. Among the casualties were the Mossend to Paris train and the three-times-weekly CTL service from Trafford Park and Willesden to Paris.

Rail freight tonnages through the tunnel recovered modestly in 2003/04, but the overall figures masked the fact that the intermodal business continued to slide. By the end of 2004 almost all the traffic to and from northern Italy

had ceased, and Intercontainer closed down its 'hub and spoke' network from Metz, which had handled some Channel Tunnel traffic. Willesden Euroterminal was quietly mothballed, its business having declined to a trickle. EWS and Transfesa failed in another attempt to open up the Silla to Dagenham automotive train to general traffic, and renewed efforts to establish an intermodal route into Germany were unsuccessful.

By the end of 2006 overall Channel Tunnel rail freight tonnages had fallen below those of 1995, the first full year of operation. Unilog withdrew its Muizen train in January 2007 after EWS had to change its pricing régime following the cessation of UK-French Government subsidies to cover the Eurotunnel 'Minimum User Charge'. Nevertheless, EWS continued to look for new business in 2007 and

On 15 July 1998 the Mossend Euroterminal pilot locomotive No 08670 shunts a rake of FIA/IFA wagons loaded with containers, most of which are carrying whisky for the French market. Whisky accounted for some 70% of the Mossend Euroterminal throughput at that time.

Despite a large downturn in business due to the asylum-seekers crisis, Hams Hall intermodal terminal still handled two Channel Tunnel flows in 2002, both to and from northern Italy. One was sponsored by Intercontainer-Interfrigo and the other by Combined Transport Limited. No 08543 stands at the head of a rake of Channel Tunnel intermodal wagons at Hams Hall on 23 October 2002.

announced that it would be launching three new routes in the following 12 months: Daventry to Brussels, Trafford Park to Duisburg, and Trafford Park to Milano. In the event, only the Trafford Park to Duisburg service got off the ground, using shared haulage with a domestic intermodal train between Trafford Park and Wembley and wagonload services between Wembley and Duisburg. The Trafford Park to Bari train ceased in 2008, having run only intermittently during the previous year.

At the start of 2009 the only Channel Tunnel intermodal services in operation were the Trafford Park to Duisburg part-trainload and a twice-weekly train from Hams Hall to Novara. The Duisburg service failed to generate sufficient business for a full trainload and was soon withdrawn. The Novara working kept going; it was diverted to run from Daventry for much of the year, but had reverted to Hams Hall by December.

Meanwhile, two new Channel Tunnel intermodal operations started during 2009. In June Colas Rail launched a twice-weekly

intermodal service between Hams Hall and Novara for Norfolk Line, initially using a Class 56 locomotive hired from Hanson Traction for the Hams Hall to Dollands Moor leg. Colas Rail had already been hauling a weekly trainload of imported steel to Burton-on-Trent via the tunnel since March, becoming the first company other than RfD or its successor EWS/DB Schenker to haul revenue-earning Channel Tunnel freight. In October DB Schenker started a weekly intermodal train for Stobart carrying refrigerated fruit and vegetables from Valencia to Dagenham, offering some compensation for losing the Transfesa Silla to Dagenham automotive flow to Colas Rail earlier in the year. This service was later diverted to serve Ripple Lane instead of Dagenham.

In late 2009 Eurotunnel's subsidiary, Europorte 2, looked set to become the third Channel Tunnel rail freight operator as it started driver-training runs for a potential intermodal service between Dourges and Daventry. The runs used a pool of Eurotunnel Class 92 locomotives that had been brought out of long-term storage and operated under First GBRf's safety case.

A mixture of Channel Tunnel and domestic traffic occupies the sidings at Trafford Park EWS terminal on 17 February 2003. At that time, the terminal had scheduled departures to Muizen, Bari, Willesden and Grangemouth.

3.

Automotive

UK car manufacturing was a thriving industry in the 1960s, with a cluster of assembly plants located in the Birmingham-Coventry area (Austin, Chrysler, Jaguar, Rover and Triumph) and others spread across the country at Dagenham (Ford), Cowley (Morris, MG and Riley), Ellesmere Port (Vauxhall), Halewood (Ford), Speke (Triumph) and Linwood

(Chrysler). By 1968 Austin, Jaguar, Morris, MG, Riley, Rover and Triumph had all merged to form British Leyland, then holding some 40% of the UK car market. Imports were relatively insignificant at that time.

As car manufacturing – and ownership – soared, so the railway seized the opportunity to distribute trainloads of cars from factories to

A lengthy rake of 'Cartic 4' wagons in their original state – before protective sides were added – forms train 4S33 from Gosford Green, Coventry, to Linwood as it passes Lostock Junction behind Class 50 No 415 on 1 June 1972. *Tom Heavyside*

Not strictly freight, but BR carried passengers' cars by train on selected routes from the 1950s onwards. The brand name 'Motorail' was adopted for this rapidly growing traffic in the mid-1960s, and at the same time BR provided a large fleet of 'Carflat' wagons converted from Mark I coach underframes. No 50050 *Fearless* passes Totnes with a well-laden Motorail train from London Paddington to St Austell on 7 August 1982. As the motorway network improved, so Motorail traffic declined and BR ran its last such train in 1995. The concept made a temporary comeback when First Great Western introduced a car-carrying service on its 'Night Riviera' sleeper train between London Paddington and Penzance in 1999; unfortunately the loadings on that service were poor and it ceased in 2005.

'Carflat' wagons conveyed commercial vehicles as well as private cars. Two early 'Carflat' designs are visible in this photograph of a trip working from Bescot to Washwood Heath, hauled by No 25263, on 31 May 1974. The location is the former Sutton Park passenger station. *Michael Mensing*

Assorted British Leyland products from Longbridge are being conveyed by train 4S34 from King's Norton to Bathgate on 13 June 1975, headed by No 45112 *Royal Army Ordnance Corps* as it passes Saltley. The train would continue its journey north via Sutton Park, Walsall and the Wolverhampton avoiding line. *Michael Mensing*

regional distribution centres and ports. Initially, cars were carried either on wagons designed for other purposes, such as steel plate carriers, or on 'Carflat' wagons converted from the underframes of redundant coaching stock. But in 1964 BR introduced its first production fleet of double-deck car-carrying wagons, offering a step change in efficiency as they could carry almost twice as many cars per unit length as a single-deck wagon. The 'Cartic 4' sets, as these new wagons were called, operated in permanently coupled sets of four, with articulated bogies except at the end of each set. They were among the first BR wagon types to be fitted with air brakes from new and later received the TOPS code XMA (subsequently changed to FQA). The

BR 'Cartics' were followed a few years later by a large privately owned fleet of similar wagons, coded PJB/PJA and operated by distributors MAT Transport, Toleman and Silcock & Colling.

The formation of British Leyland in 1968 resulted in the pooling of manufacturing facilities, which produced some valuable railborne flows of components such as Austin-Morris engines from Longbridge to Cowley and Abingdon, body panels from Pressed Steel Fisher at Swindon to Longbridge and Abingdon, and completed bodies from Cowley to the Birmingham area for Triumph, Rover and Jaguar. The Swindon to Longbridge flow was particularly large, with nine trains a week each comprising 24 air-braked pallet vans. Finished

British Leyland cars were loaded at several sites in the Birmingham area including the Longbridge factory and railheads at Knowle & Dorridge and King's Norton. The destinations included ports such as Dover and Harwich as well as domestic terminals at Bathgate, Wrenthorpe (Wakefield) and Teesside.

Ford was a major user of rail transport, with extensive sidings at its main factories. BR carried regular trainloads of components between Halewood and Dagenham, using electric haulage between Halewood and Willesden. This was ideal rail traffic because the wagons could be loaded both ways, carrying gearboxes from Halewood and engines from Dagenham. The railway also moved transmissions from Ford's Swansea plant to both Halewood and Dagenham. Finished cars were distributed by rail from Halewood and Dagenham in both wagonload and trainload quantities, with destinations including Maidenhead, Exeter, Bell Green (Coventry), Wrenthorpe and Garston. Southampton-built Transit vans were loaded at Eastleigh from the early 1970s onwards.

No 82004 heads an eastbound trainload of Ford Escorts near Aston on the freight-only line to Stechford on 6 June 1975. This service normally ran via the West Coast Main Line but had been diverted via Bescot, Aston and Stechford because of an overnight crash at Nuneaton. *Michael Mensing*

Dagenham: block car train departures, May 1976			
Code	Dep	Days	Destination
4M41	0050	ThSO	Garston
4M30	1355	SX	Garston
4S42	1955	TThO	Elderslie
4L44	2300	MWFO	Wrenthorpe

Garston/Ditton: block car train departures, May 1977			
Code	Dep	Days	Destination
4O41	0138	TThSO	Newhaven
4E42	1237	MThO	Dagenham
4O55	1237	TWFO	Eastleigh
4S41	2120	MWFO	Elderslie
4E36	2120	TThO	Wrenthorpe
4E38	2205	SX	Dagenham

Washwood Heath area: block car train departures, May 1975			
Code	Dep	Days	Origin and destination
4O31	0015	TThSO	Dorridge-Dover
4E34	0015	WFO	Dorridge-Harwich
4E32	0155	TThO	King's Norton-Wakefield
4E32	0752	SO	King's Norton-Wakefield
4E32	1917	ThSX	King's Norton-Tyneside Central FD
4O30	2145	TThO	King's Norton-Lenham

As for the other UK manufacturers, Vauxhall made relatively little use of rail, while Chrysler generated regular traffic in containers between Gosford Green (Coventry) and Linwood, with Hillman Imp and Hunter engines travelling north and Avenger body panels, axles and gearboxes returning south. Finished cars were conveyed on the same Anglo-Scottish route.

After peaking at just over 1.9 million vehicles in 1972, UK car production was dogged by persistent industrial disputes and entered a period of sharp decline, falling below one million by the end of the decade. Some plants closed altogether:

Ford provided the railway with high-volume flows of both cars and components between its Dagenham and Merseyside plants. No 86033 passes Apsley with 7E39, the 0600 train from Halewood to Dagenham, on 21 July 1983. At that time the component traffic was carried in several different types of van, including VQB pallet vans with their distinctive panelled sides. The train pictured here also includes two OBA open wagons.

Cars from various locations in the UK were railed to Stranraer for shipment to Northern Ireland, using general Speedlink services via Carlisle and Ayr. No 08727 shunts an empty 'Procor 80' PLA wagon at Stranraer Harbour on 25 July 1985.

the main Triumph assembly line at Speke closed in 1978 and Chrysler's Linwood factory eked out a precarious existence until 1981. As car ownership continued to rise, so the proportion of imported vehicles increased from just 7% in 1970 to 34% in 1980. The railway catered for

With a lengthy rake of 'Cartic 4' PJA wagons in tow, No 86030 departs from Speke Junction with 6E42, the 1234 Ford company train from Garston to Dagenham on 1 April 1986. Trains on this route often ran loaded in both directions, making this a highly cost-effective operation.

Passing the derelict St Albans South signal box, which had closed eight years previously, No 31423 heads south with 7A40, the 1657 Luton Crescent Road to Willesden Speedlink trip working, on 8 July 1987. The Vauxhall vans and cars were destined for Bathgate and would travel north on an overnight service from Willesden. St Albans City signal box had been designated a listed building and was later painstakingly restored as a heritage attraction.

The wiring up of the North London line in 1988 enabled through electric working between the West Coast Main Line and North Thameside. The first trains to take advantage of this investment were the Ford automotive workings between Dagenham and Garston. No 85016 passes Highbury & Islington with the 1245 departure from Dagenham on 7 July 1988.

the rise in imports by setting up trainload flows from various ports, backed up by the Speedlink network for smaller-scale deliveries. Some examples of new import traffic were Datsun cars from Eastleigh to Leyburn (Wensleydale) in 1978, more Japanese products from Lowestoft in 1979, and short-term flows from Hartlepool Docks to Elderslie, Cowley and Hayes & Harlington in 1981.

The fleet of car-carrying wagons was boosted by several new designs in the late 1970s and early 1980s. First came the 'Procor 80' wagon, a double-deck design based on the 'Cartic 4' sets but consisting of single wagons mounted on individual bogies rather than permanently coupled sets of four. Originally coded PLA (later JLA), the 'Procor 80' overcame a major disadvantage of the 'Cartic 4' that, if one wagon failed, the whole set of four wagons was out of

use. The 'Procor 80' also offered greater flexibility for smaller-scale loads, especially those using the Speedlink network, and its more generous headroom on the lower deck allowed larger cars to be carried than on a 'Cartic'. Among the work assigned to the 'Procor 80s' were movements of imported Renaults from Goole and various makes from Harwich to Bathgate for the distributor Toleman.

In 1981 the PKA 'Autic' wagon made its appearance. Built by SNAV in France, the 'Autic' was a two-part double-deck vehicle mounted on just three axles, with a less pronounced dip in the centre of the deck thanks to the use of single axles with small wheels instead of bogies. Another useful feature of the 'Autic' was that its upper deck ends were hinged to form a ramp and allow loading from platform level, obviating the need for a high-level ramp at the railhead.

'Autics' were used on a wide range of flows, including imported cars from Queenborough and Goole and British Leyland products from King's Norton.

Also introduced in 1981 was the PQA 'Comtic', essentially a single-deck version of the 'Autic', which could carry commercial vehicles as well as cars with a taller than usual profile. These wagons worked alongside, and to some extent replaced, traditional 'Carflats'. A number of 'Comtics' were later adapted for train ferry operation and carried the code PIA.

During the 1980s BR retained a number of significant domestic and export flows such as British Leyland (later Austin Rover) cars from Longbridge and Cowley, Ford cars from Dagenham and Halewood (loaded at Garston), and Transit vans from Eastleigh. Vauxhall returned to rail for a time, using Luton Crescent Road freight terminal as a loading point. The biggest import flow comprised European Fords from Dover, including some 'land bridge' traffic for Northern Ireland via Stranraer. Wherever possible, flows for the domestic market were directed to a small number of large distribution terminals, such as the MAT facility at Bathgate,

Above left **Conveying approximately 200 Metro and Maestro cars on MAT 'Cartic' wagons, No 47599 leaves the Austin Rover sidings complex at Longbridge with the 4T53 trip working to Washwood Heath on 13 August 1987. At Washwood Heath, trip workings from Longbridge fed into trunk trains to Dover, Harwich and Bathgate.**

Left **The Volkswagen and Audi group used Wolverton distribution terminal as a railhead for imports of spare parts from Germany. No 31455 sets out from Wolverton with empty vans on 23 August 1989 forming 6O82, the 1755 company train to Dover. Access to and from the distribution terminal was by means of the dive-under line in the centre of the picture.**

which benefited from major investment at the start of the decade. Component traffic included a new flow of engines from the Ford plant at Bridgend, which opened in 1980.

A sad development in the 1980s was the targeting of car trains by stone-throwers. The railway responded by fitting side screens and roofs to many car-carrying wagons, altering their appearance substantially. Many of the 'Cartics' operated by MAT gained mesh metal screens, while Silcock preferred off-white solid plastic panels. Some 'Autics' received similar modifications.

When BR was divided into business sectors, it made good sense for automotive traffic to come under the Railfreight Distribution (RfD) umbrella. A number of automotive flows used the Speedlink network and, with construction of the Channel Tunnel under way, BR was keen to develop automotive traffic between the UK and mainland Europe. BR's confidence in the Channel Tunnel was great enough for it to set up a joint venture with Silcock Express with the intention of building three distribution terminals in the UK for cars imported through the tunnel, located in the South East, the West Midlands and the Central Belt of Scotland.

BR also ordered from Arbel Fauvet Rail a fleet of 300 totally enclosed car-carrying wagons for Channel Tunnel traffic, permanently coupled in sets of five. Apart from eliminating the risk of vandalism, the use of totally enclosed wagons meant that cars would no longer need to be waxed before delivery, leading to savings of time and money. The wagons would be operated by Autocare Europe, a new joint venture partnership between RfD, Belgian National Railways, Ferry-Boats and Cobelfret.

RfD Automotive timetable, October 1993

Code	Dep	Days	Origin and destination
6M78	2230	SX	Bridgend-Newport ADJ-Halewood-Garston
6M41	0120	MX	Dagenham-Garston
4O12	0314	MX	Dagenham-Eastleigh
6M37	1203	SX	Dagenham-Garston
6V30	2211	SX	Dagenham-Newport ADJ
4L40	1601	SX	Eastleigh-Dagenham
6V91	1900	SX	Garston-Halewood-Newport ADJ-Bridgend
6L42	1240	SX	Garston-Dagenham
6L48	2120	SX	Garston-Dagenham
4V07	0205	MSX	Longbridge-Morris Cowley
6V27	0450	MSX	Longbridge-Swindon
6V09	0550	MO	Longbridge-Swindon
4T55	0620	SX	Longbridge-Washwood Heath
6V22	1215	SX	Longbridge-Swindon
4V05	1330	FSX	Longbridge-Morris Cowley
4T53	1430	SX	Longbridge-Washwood Heath
4G17	2058	FO	Longbridge-Washwood Heath
6V41	2130	FSX	Longbridge-Swindon
4T54	2255	SX	Longbridge-Washwood Heath
4O20	0730	MSX	Morris Cowley-Southampton Docks
4M01	0830	MO	Morris Cowley-Washwood Heath
4M09	2015	FSX	Morris Cowley-Longbridge
4M09	2015	FO	Morris Cowley-Washwood Heath
6L46	0150	MX	Newport ADJ-Dagenham
6B10	0700	MX	Newport ADJ-Swansea Burrows
6C46	0717	SO	Newport ADJ-Swansea Burrows
4M43	0344	MX	Parkeston-Washwood Heath
4M44	1226	SX	Parkeston-Washwood Heath
4M03	2244	MSX	Parkeston-Washwood Heath
4M04	1528	MSX	Southampton Docks-Washwood Heath
6B14	1850	SX	Swansea Burrows-Newport ADJ
6M37	0155	SX	Swindon-Longbridge
6M03	0140	SX	Swindon-Longbridge
6M08	1820	FSX	Swindon-Longbridge
4T53	0145	MSX	Washwood Heath-Longbridge
4V07	0315	SO	Washwood Heath-Morris Cowley
4L39	0830	MSX	Washwood Heath-Ely-Parkeston
4T53	1050	SX	Washwood Heath-Longbridge
4T52	1600	SX	Washwood Heath-Tyseley-Bordesley-Washwood Heath
4L34	2008	SX	Washwood Heath-Parkeston
4L37	2351	SX	Washwood Heath-Ely-Parkeston

Domestic movements for Rover (formerly British Leyland) decreased in 1992 when the service to Bathgate was withdrawn, but received a boost in the following year when RfD set up a new distribution railhead at Ely in conjunction with the Potter Group and Midland Car Distributors. This was a surprising gain in view of the short distance between the West Midlands and Ely, but the Ely terminal was attractive to Rover because it offered a 25-acre site for stockpiling cars and RfD could provide the rail service cheaply by tacking Ely wagons on to scheduled trains to Harwich.

The train plan for Rover at that time was relatively complex, catering for traffic from three loading terminals – Longbridge, Bordesley and Cowley – to four destinations – Cowley,

Southampton, Ely and Harwich. Most trains were routed to or from Washwood Heath yard, which had lost its general freight marshalling role in the 1970s but was well placed geographically to handle the Rover business. The busiest of the receiving terminals was Harwich, which received three trainloads from Washwood Heath each weekday. Two of those trains also called at Ely on their outward journey. Trains to Cowley and Southampton were organised to take account of the fact that Cowley was both a receiving terminal and a factory railhead. One daily diagram was a straightforward out-and-back working between Longbridge and Cowley, carrying mainly southbound traffic but sometimes also backloaded with cars for onward transit to Ely and Harwich. The other diagram operated

Bordesley was used as a loading point for various car producers in the West Midlands, including Land Rover at Solihull. Still coupled to the ramp wagon that was used to load cars on the upper deck, No 08692 positions an articulated PQA wagon in the departure sidings at Bordesley on 22 May 1987. This wagon would be combined with the rake of single-deck wagons in the adjacent siding to form a trip working to Washwood Heath.

Transit vans from the Ford plant at Swaythling were conveyed by rail using a mixture of block trains and general wagonload freight services. No 47326 approaches Pirbright Junction with the 1557 Eastleigh to Dagenham train on 17 July 1992, conveying vans bound for Garston on a combination of PKA 'Comtic' and FVA/FVW 'Cartic' wagons. This traffic had been conveyed by a direct Eastleigh to Garston train until the May 1992 timetable change.

in triangular fashion four days a week, running loaded from Longbridge to Cowley, loaded from Cowley to Southampton, and empty from Southampton to Washwood Heath. On the fifth day it ran only between Washwood Heath and Cowley.

The heavy traffic in body panels from Swindon to Longbridge was given a new lease of life in February 1994 when BR renewed its contract with Rover for five years. The contract was marked by the naming of Class 47 No 47323 as *Rover Group Quality Assured*. RfD operated up to three daily trainloads from Swindon to Longbridge, using internationally registered Cargowaggon vans. Some £100,000 was invested

in new trackwork at Swindon and the trains were rerouted via Oxford instead of Cheltenham in order to avoid the need for banking on the Lickey Incline. Two years later, RfD would introduce purpose-built KSA 'high cube' wagons on this traffic, enabling even larger loads to be carried thanks to the cargo hold between their bogies, accessed by an electrically operated sliding floor.

BR's first contract for Channel Tunnel automotive traffic was a three-year deal covering exports of Rover cars from Longbridge to Arluno in northern Italy. The flow actually began in March 1994 and used the Dover to Dunkerque train ferry until the tunnel was ready. In due course it was a Longbridge to Arluno train that provided the tunnel with its first revenue-earning freight on 1 June 1994. Before long the service amounted to five trains a week. Each train conveyed some 200 cars and was more than 2,000 feet long, making it the UK's longest automotive formation. However, the Arluno service did not use the fully enclosed wagons that had been designed for tunnel traffic; instead it used conventional 'Cartic'-type stock that

Vauxhall car and van traffic from Luton saw a brief revival in the 1990s, when Railfreight Distribution introduced a direct block train to Bathgate. No 47237 shunts an assortment of single- and double-deck wagons at Luton on 25 July 1994 before departing with 4S48, the 1745 service to Bathgate.

Railfreight Distribution's fleet of fully enclosed car carrying wagons, coded WIA for TOPS purposes, provided the automotive industry with the ultimate defence against vandalism and accidental damage during transit. However, they were not fully utilised on Channel Tunnel flows and many WIAs were either stored for long periods or used on domestic flows. No 90137 passes Rugby on 21 July 1995 with a mixture of WIAs and other wagon types forming train 6M37, the 1203 from Dagenham to Garston.

was adapted for Channel Tunnel use. Initially all Arluno trains returned empty to the UK, but later RfD was able to backload one train a week with Fiat cars from northern Italy to Avonmouth.

The second automotive flow to use the tunnel was component traffic for Ford. RfD signed a major contract with Transfesa in January 1994 for a daily trainload of Ford components between Valencia in Spain and Ford's UK factories. The trains conveyed swapbodies on a fleet of French-registered IFB two-axle wagons that had variable-gauge axles for standard and Spanish track gauges as well as conforming to the various tunnel profile limitations of Spain, France and the UK. The original intention was for the train to serve Ford factories at Dagenham, Halewood and in South Wales, but in the event it only ran to and from Dagenham.

A domestic gain for RfD in 1994 was Vauxhall car and van traffic from Luton to Bathgate, which had been moving by road for several years. A three-year contract with MAT Transauto and Mainland Car Deliveries Limited provided for three trains a week, routed via Washwood Heath and the West Coast Main Line. Unfortunately, that contract was cut short and the traffic ceased in the spring of 1995. The Bathgate terminal remained open for seasonal deliveries of Peugeots from Calais.

The year 1995 also brought the demise of Rover traffic from the West Midlands to Harwich and Ely. The main reason for this loss was Rover's decision to ship cars to mainland Europe from Purfleet instead of Harwich; the Ely business was not viable as a stand-alone operation.

Scottish traffic received a boost in 1995 when Autotrax, a joint venture between RfD and Axial, took over two of the six tracks in Mossend Euroterminal to provide an automotive railhead.

Operationally, Mossend was a more favourable location than Bathgate as it lay on the electrified West Coast Main Line. Its initial business included Ford cars and vans from Dagenham, Garston and Eastleigh.

In 1996 GEFCO opened its rail-served distribution depot at Corby, which received trainloads of Peugeot and Citroën cars from France via the Channel Tunnel. These trains comprised traffic from four different factories, assembled into trainloads at Achères yard near Paris. GEFCO also delivered some cars by rail to Doncaster Railport. More new business for the Channel Tunnel came from Ford, which set up a daily service from Genk to Garston for Mondeo cars. The Genk train used some of the fully enclosed WIA wagons, which had so far been woefully under-deployed.

Once RfD joined the EWS fold in November 1997, the rail automotive business enjoyed a period of expansion, with various new flows either operating by the trainload or taking advantage of the growing Enterprise wagonload network. The GEFCO traffic to Corby reached a maximum of eight trains a week in the summer of 1998. As well as using the Channel Tunnel, GEFCO put some cars on rail at Sheerness, where a loading terminal in the port area had been restored to use. By the end of 1998 EWS had run trial or short-term flows of Daewoo cars from Avonmouth to Mossend, Nissan cars from Doncaster to Italy, Mazda cars from

Autotrax established a car terminal within the Mossend Euroterminal compound in 1995. The traffic included home-produced Ford cars and vans from Dagenham, Halewood and Eastleigh, as well as various consignments of imported vehicles. On 15 July 1998 Ford Escorts and Couriers are being unloaded at Mossend from a rake of French-registered IFA former steel-carrying wagons, now converted for automotive use and permanently coupled in sets of four.

Final securing and checking takes place before another load of Land Rover products is ready to leave Bordesley on 23 February 2001. The ambitious plans that were made to build a railway link to the Land Rover plant unfortunately came to nothing, and Land Rover stopped using rail altogether in 2002.

Doncaster Railport became a receiving and loading point for various automotive flows. No 08514 pulls a rake of empty IPA wagons out of the Railport access siding on 29 May 2007. This was a trip working to Belmont yard, which would use the flyover to cross the East Coast Main Line and run round at St Catherine's Junction before returning on the 'down' side to Belmont.

Queenborough to Selby and Glasgow Deanside, Renault cars from Southampton to Teesport, Land Rovers from Bordesley to Southampton, Ford Transit vans from Immingham to Dagenham and Avonmouth, and Case tractors from Doncaster to France.

While EWS expanded its car-carrying business, Freightliner entered the automotive market with the launch of its 'Autoliner' operation, using collapsible 'Car Rac' platforms that could be carried on Freightliner wagons. By the end of 1999 Freightliner had moved its first cars and was well on the way to gaining a share of the Ford traffic from Dagenham and Southampton to Garston and Mossend.

Investment projects announced during 1999 included the building of a new automotive and intermodal terminal at Tyne Dock, supported by a Government grant of nearly £700,000. Tyne Dock became the loading point for Nissan traffic to Italy, with a weekly train operating by the summer of 1999. Tyne Dock also received a weekly train from Avonmouth from early 2000, carrying container-loads of Nissan components from Spain. Meanwhile, a £315,000 grant supported the provision of a new Rover loading terminal at Cowley, the previous traffic from Cowley having ceased in 1997. An even bigger project on the horizon was a £40 million proposal by Land Rover to build a 2½-mile rail link to its

The Rover component trains from Swindon to Longbridge were rostered for double-headed Class 47 traction in 1998 in order to improve their reliability. Nos 47241 and 47285 pass Bordesley with 4M08, the 1415 Swindon to Longbridge train, on 10 June 1998.

Solihull plant. Unfortunately, that project never came to fruition.

The resumption of Rover traffic from Cowley was short-lived as Rover 75 production switched to Longbridge in 2000. But the Cowley branch was assured a future as the plant became the production site for the new BMW Mini. In 2001 EWS introduced a daily trainload of Minis from Cowley to Purfleet for export, using fully enclosed WIA wagons. Meanwhile, Vauxhall experimented with rail again, using Ellesmere Port as a loading point for trainloads of Astra estate cars to Purfleet from early 2000. Unfortunately the Vauxhall traffic used open wagons and too many cars were vandalised for the business to be sustainable.

Jaguar made a major commitment to rail when it installed new loading facilities at Halewood, supported by a £1.8 million Government grant. The first loaded train left the new terminal in April 2001, bound for Southampton Docks in fully enclosed WIA wagons. Jaguar's sister plant at Castle Bromwich would gain a rail connection in the following year, part-funded by a £5.3 million grant and again producing traffic for export via Southampton. Previously some of the Castle Bromwich product had been conveyed by rail from Bordesley.

Automotive traffic played a part in two line reopenings in 2001-02. One was the long-mooted revival of the former Portishead branch to serve coal and automotive import terminals at Royal Portbury Dock. By 2002 Portbury was generating intermittent car trains to Bathgate, carrying a mixture of

Under Jaguar ownership, Halewood car factory had its rail connection reactivated for daily consignments of cars for export via Southampton. No 66092 departs from the loading area at Halewood with the first loaded train of Jaguars on 23 April 2001.

makes including Vauxhall, Toyota and Fiat. The other addition to the network was the former colliery branch to Baddesley, which was relaid in 2002 to serve the TNT Logistics/Volkswagen parts distribution centre at Birch Coppice. EWS introduced a daily trip working from Bescot to Birch Coppice to deliver vanloads of parts from Germany.

During 2002 Freightliner Heavy Haul confirmed its presence in the automotive market with regular services carrying Ford vehicles from Dagenham and Southampton to Garston and Mossend, as well as occasional import traffic from Portbury. Freightliner also made trial movements on other routes, such as Corby to Garston and Grimsby to Corby, but these failed to develop into regular business. The various flows from Dagenham, Southampton and Portbury made use of Freightliner's curtain-sided 'Autoflat' wagons – essentially purpose-built containers mounted on standard intermodal wagons – which offered protection from stone chippings and

The first traffic to use the reopened Birch Coppice branch was an automotive component flow for Volkswagen, using IZA twin vans that were tripped from Bescot yard up to five times a week. Unimog road-rail vehicle No 9210 shunts a rake of loaded vans towards the headshunt at Birch Coppice on 22 August 2006, before setting back into the TNT Logistics depot visible on the left. Unfortunately this traffic switched to road haulage in late 2007.

No 66110 passes Narroways Hill Junction, Bristol, with train 6X52, the 1727 from Portbury to Washwood Heath, on 3 June 2008. This train conveyed imported vans on IFA and IPA flat wagons and connected with an onward service from Washwood Heath to Tyne Dock.

Freightliner began handling automotive traffic as one of the first steps towards diversification from its core intermodal business, but ultimately the profit margins were too small and the traffic was relinquished. No 47150 passes South Kenton with 6M26, the 1405 Dagenham to Crewe train, on 15 July 2002.

The IFB/IFA wagons carrying component traffic between Silla and Dagenham were restricted to 45mph on the British side of the Channel and the trains were therefore designated Class 7. No 47360 pulls out of the Ford sidings at Dagenham with train 7M05, the 1534 departure to Wembley, on 29 October 1998. The down sidings visible on the left were used for car loading at that time, but later became the railhead for domestic refuse traffic to Calvert.

vandals. For a time these flows seemed to thrive under Freightliner management, but in 2005 Freightliner pulled out of automotive traffic completely after Fiat cancelled its distribution contract with Freightliner's customer Walon and after Ford revamped its whole distribution strategy.

Meanwhile the collapse of Rover in 2005, following the failure of a proposed joint venture with China, brought an abrupt end to EWS's long-standing traffic from Longbridge. The

Swindon to Longbridge body panel flow had already ceased in the previous year, leaving the specialised fleet of KSA 'high cube' wagons looking for new work. Another loss in 2005 was Ford component traffic from Swansea to Dagenham, leaving just Bridgend on the South Wales axis.

The year 2007 saw the closure of Bathgate as an automotive railhead, with Tyne Dock taking over as the receiving terminal for imported cars from Portbury. This change allowed some wagons to be backloaded more easily with Nissan cars from Tyne Dock to Portbury. Channel Tunnel automotive traffic had sunk to a low level by this time, with just the imports of Peugeot cars to Corby and components from Silla to Dagenham. A welcome development, therefore, was the commencement of Honda traffic from South Marston to Gent via the Channel Tunnel in 2007, using fully enclosed WIA wagons.

A decisive sign of the decline in West Midlands car manufacturing was the closure of Washwood Heath yard in late 2008. For many years it had been an important staging point for automotive traffic but, following the closure of Longbridge and the loss of Peugeot traffic

Colas Rail was the first freight operator to challenge the monopoly of EWS in the Channel Tunnel rail freight market. The trains were hauled to and from Dollands Moor by various types of traction: Colas Class 47, Riviera Trains Class 47, Hanson Traction Class 56 and, once they became available, Colas Class 66. Hanson Traction loco No 56311 weaves through Ripple Lane yard with 7Z98, the 0520 Ford/Transfesa train from Dollands Moor to Dagenham, on 27 August 2009.

from Bordesley, EWS could no longer justify maintaining a facility to marshal automotive trains in the West Midlands. Trains to and from Castle Bromwich could be staged at Bescot instead of Washwood Heath, and long-distance flows such as Portbury to Tyne Yard or Mossend could operate throughout as a block train.

Further cutbacks in the DB Schenker (former EWS) network led to some automotive trains being diverted to call at Warrington instead of Bescot in early 2010. This change involved rerouteing the import flow from Portbury to Mossend via the West Coast Main Line, with a connecting service operating from Warrington to Doncaster Railport. By this time some long-established automotive flows had disappeared from the network, including Peugeot imports to Corby and Ford traffic from Southampton. Doubtless the recession was partly to blame for the traffic losses; hopes were high that an economic recovery would bring a revival for railborne car movements and, in particular, for Channel Tunnel traffic, which had once looked to be such a safe bet for the railway.

4.

Chemicals

Caustic soda, carbon dioxide, sulphuric acid, liquid chlorine, ethylene dibromide, styrene monomer… These were just a few of the chemicals that were transported in bulk by rail in the UK in the 1970s and 1980s. Today, chemicals trains are almost an extinct species on the British rail network, partly because of the restructuring of the chemical industry, with fewer opportunities to move large quantities of chemicals between plants, and partly because most of what remains on rail has been switched to intermodal operation.

Chemicals traffic became more conspicuous in the 1960s as major manufacturers such as ICI and BP introduced fleets of specialised tank wagons, often brightly coloured and often running in block train formations between key sites. The investment in rail continued into the 1970s and 1980s, with some companies tapping into the Government Section 8 Grant scheme to provide new wagons and better terminal facilities. The Speedlink wagonload network catered for many smaller-scale chemicals flows and sometimes acted as a nursery for potential trainload traffic. The demise of Speedlink in 1991 deprived the chemicals industry of some useful flexibility and left most potential rail freight customers with an 'all or nothing' situation – either they had to invest in a free-standing trainload operation right from the start, or they could not use rail at all. The limited revival of wagonload freight under Transrail and EWS did cater for a few chemicals flows, but by 2009 any new business was being handled on a strictly trainload-only basis.

Teesside was one of the country's biggest centres for railborne chemicals traffic in the 1970s and 1980s. On the north side of the Tees, Haverton Hill yard served the massive ICI Billingham plant. BR ran block trains of anhydrous ammonia from Haverton Hill to Barton-on-Humber, Severn Beach, Heysham, Leith and Grangemouth. The ammonia was used to manufacture fertilisers and was carried in white- or grey-liveried bogie tanks with a horizontal orange band, with various TOPS codes including TCA, TDA and TIB. Another block train service carried hydrocyanic acid, an ingredient in the manufacturing of synthetic fibres, from Grangemouth to Haverton Hill. A short-distance flow of hydrocyanic acid also operated from Seal Sands to Haverton Hill. Because of the high toxicity of this substance, these trains always included two heavyweight barrier wagons at each end of the formation, together with a brake-van at the rear. Haverton Hill also produced various wagonload flows of chemicals including methanol, carbon dioxide, urea and amines. Seal Sands generated various wagonload and trainload flows of chemicals, including a twice-weekly block train to the UKF fertiliser plant at Ince & Elton and inward trainloads of sulphuric acid from St Helens. On the south side of the Tees, ICI Wilton dispatched a daily trainload of cyclohexane to Stevenston alongside wagonload flows of chemicals such as adipic acid and pure terephthalic acid.

The railway served chemicals plants on both sides of the Humber estuary. On the north side, BP Chemicals at Saltend produced trainloads of acetic acid to Baglan Bay and Saltend, as well as various wagonload flows. On the south bank of the Humber the ports of Immingham and Grimsby produced a number of rail flows, including imported caustic soda and acrylonitrile. The Fisons works at Immingham was one of several East Coast sites that sent out packaged

The BP plant at Saltend, Hull, produced acetic acid, which was conveyed by rail to Baglan Bay, Spondon and Seal Sands. No 37217 passes Toton on 23 April 1990 with 6E19, the 1710 Spondon to Doncaster Speedlink train, conveying six empty acetic acid tanks and two empty fuel oil tanks.

Type 2 (later Class 25) locomotive No D5155 descends Wilpshire bank with empty PCV soda ash tanks returning to ICI Northwich on 20 April 1968. These tanks had entered service only two years earlier but would soon become obsolete as BR adopted air instead of vacuum brakes for new rolling-stock builds. *Gavin Morrison*

The BP Chemicals plant at Sandbach dispatched liquid chlorine by rail both by the wagonload and in full trainloads. No 40180 winds out of Basford Hall sidings, Crewe, with a southbound train of liquid chlorine on 4 April 1979. *Gavin Morrison*

Above **In later years ICI used bogie tank wagons for its flows of anhydrous ammonia from Haverton Hill. No 47225 passes Norton East box as it comes off the freight-only line from Ferryhill with train 6E74, the 0944 empty tanks from Leith South to Haverton Hill, on 18 July 1986.**

Below **The Leathers chemical works at St Helens continued to provide traffic for the rump of the former through line between St Helens Shaw Street and St Helens Junction, which was taken out of use south of Ravenhead Junction in January 1989. No 31147 propels two sulphuric acid tanks past Ravenhead Junction box on 15 February 1989, having formed a trip working from Warrington Arpley.**

fertiliser by rail in the 1970s, mainly loaded in vacuum-braked vans that used the national wagonload network. The Courtaulds rayon plant at Grimsby received trainloads of caustic soda from Runcorn.

In North West England, the presence of large underground salt deposits had led to a thriving chemical industry. The railway served several major plants in Cheshire including ICI at Northwich (Winnington, Wallerscote and Lostock), BP at Sandbach, British Salt at Middlewich, ICI at Runcorn, UKF at Ince & Elton, and Shell and

Top **Hydrocyanic acid was such a dangerous substance that trains carrying it had to include two purpose-built barrier wagons at the front and rear as well as a brake-van. No 37147 rounds the curve at Newton Hall, just north of Durham, with train 6X99, the 2338 Grangemouth to Haverton Hill, on 14 May 1982.**

Middle **BR carried block trains of anhydrous ammonia from the ICI plant at Haverton Hill to several destinations including Heysham, Leith and Severn Beach. The Heysham traffic was carried in vacuum-braked TTV/TTF two-axle tank wagons, flanked by barrier vans and with a brake-van at the rear. No 40150 enters Heysham Moss sidings with 7M37, the 0340 from Haverton Hill to Heysham, on 11 July 1983.**

Bottom **The ICI complex at Haverton Hill was once a major user of rail freight, with exchange sidings and an extensive internal railway system reached by a spur from Belasis Lane on the Seal Sands branch. No 47207 passes Belasis Lane box with 6O49, the 1600 Haverton Hill to Eastleigh Speedlink train, on 16 July 1986. At that time Haverton Hill produced block train departures to Leith South, Grangemouth, Glazebrook and Runcorn Folly Lane, and was also the starting point for Speedlink trains to Warrington Arpley and Eastleigh.**

Associated Octel at Ellesmere Port.

The ICI complex at Northwich produced large quantities of soda ash, also known as sodium carbonate, for use by the glass and detergent industries, and BR played a major part in its distribution. Most of the soda ash was conveyed in railway-owned covered hopper wagons and used the wagonload network, but in the 1970s ICI leased several fleets of air-braked rolling stock and greater use was made of block trains. From 1975 the flow of soda ash from Northwich to Albright & Wilson at Corkickle benefited from a fleet of pressure-discharge tanks with bodies that could be tilted during unloading, coded TTA (later PEA) for TOPS purposes. More conventional PCA tank wagons were introduced on a trainload flow to Larbert and on Speedlink traffic to Barnby Dun and Knottingley.

The BP works at Sandbach (Elworth), formerly owned by Murgatroyds, was a long-

Below **ICI hired a unique fleet of 'Tip Air' tanks to carry sodium carbonate from its Lostock works to Albright & Wilson at Corkickle. Coded PEA for TOPS purposes, the 'Tip Air' tanks could be tilted to enable the lightweight load to be discharged satisfactorily. No 40057 passes Silverdale with 6F58, the 1451 Corkickle to Northwich empties, on 14 July 1983.**

standing user of rail. In the 1970s it dispatched tankloads of liquid chlorine to Esso at Fawley and to BP at Baglan Bay. The works also produced caustic soda, hydrochloric acid and sodium hypochlorite. Also reached by the Sandbach to Northwich freight-only line was the British Salt works at Middlewich, which produced mainly wagonload traffic.

ICI's Runcorn complex provided plenty of business for the short freight-only Folly Lane branch, and even justified the electrification of that branch when the Crewe to Liverpool line was energised. The Runcorn plant was best known for its production of caustic soda, but it also produced various chlorinated hydrocarbons such as perchloroethylene and sodium hyperchlorite. In the early 1980s BR still ran block trains from Folly Lane to Holywell Junction, Burn Naze, Corkickle, Immingham, Grimsby, Seal Sands, Stevenston and Willesden, as well as wagonload traffic to other destinations.

The Shellstar (later UKF) fertiliser plant at Ince & Elton invested heavily in rail in 1968 when it acquired its first purpose-built air-braked vans to carry bagged fertiliser to various railheads around the country. By the mid-1970s UKF owned or leased a total of 90 vans, coded PWA for TOPS purposes, and operated an

Above **Block trains of soda ash ran from Oakleigh to a distribution railhead at Larbert until 1993, using PCA wagons hired from Procor. No 85102 heads south near Oxenholme with 6M27, the 0631 Larbert to Oakleigh empty tank train, on 21 July 1990.**

intricate network of company trains as listed in the accompanying table. Although these were company trains, they often carried portions for two or more destinations. The inclusion of weekend departures enabled the wagon fleet to be utilised as efficiently as possible, with some vehicles clocking up three round trips a week. UKF also used the wagonload and Speedlink networks to serve smaller terminals. Alongside the fertiliser trains, UKF dispatched anhydrous

Below **With the 2273-foot summit of Pen-y-Ghent dominating the skyline, No 40169 whistles north with a short rake of caustic soda tanks on 20 July 1982. The train is 6S35, the 1530 from Burn Naze to Stevenston.**

ammonia to Barton-on-Humber and nitric acid to Thames Haven, and received phosphoric acid from Avonmouth, Immingham and, later, Corkickle.

Ellesmere Port yard was the gathering point for traffic to and from two short branches of the Manchester Ship Canal Railway, one serving the Unitank and Pan-Ocean tank farms at Eastham and the other serving Shell Chemicals and Associated

Ince UKF fertiliser train plan, October 1978					
Code	Dep	Days	From	To	Traffic also for
6S89	1230	WO	Ince & Elton	Keith	Aberdeen, Montrose, Kirkcaldy
6E40	1512	SuO	Ince & Elton	Braintree	Whittlesea, Lincoln, Dereham, Diss, Ipswich, Sandy
6V35	1530	SO	Ince & Elton	Carmarthen	Gloucester
6E40	1607	MTWO	Ince & Elton	Whitemoor	Whittlesea, Lincoln, Sleaford, Dereham, Diss, Ipswich, Sandy
6O48	1630	FO	Ince & Elton	Horsham	Akeman Street
6V35	1709	SuO	Ince & Elton	Truro	Plymouth, Lapford
6V35	1728	TO	Ince & Elton	Plymouth	Bridgwater
6O34	1728	ThO	Ince & Elton	Andover	Gillingham
6E56	2020	MO	Ince & Elton	Darlington	Harrogate

UKF introduced its own air-braked pallet vans in 1968 and set up a network of regional distribution terminals to receive block trains of fertiliser from its manufacturing plant at Ince & Elton. The Speedlink network was also used for some destinations. No 47041 passes Dunning with empty fertiliser vans returning to Ince & Elton on 20 July 1984, forming 6O56, the 1510 from Dundee to Dover Town. The Ince & Elton plant stopped sending fertiliser by rail in the early 1990s.

Octel. The Unitank and Pan-Ocean tank farms handled a wide variety of traffic over the years, mainly in wagonload quantities. Traffic from Shell Chemicals included alcohols to Grangemouth, acetone to the Royal Ordnance Factory at Bishopton and acetone to Glaxo at Plumpton Junction. Associated Octel generated daily rail freight movements between its main

The Associated Octel plant at Amlwch kept the 17-mile Gaerwen to Amlwch branch open for nearly three decades after its closure to passengers in 1964. No 47128 poses just outside the plant, on the short stretch of light railway that was built in 1952, ready to depart with train 7D05, the 0825 to Llandudno Junction, on 18 April 1985. The payload includes four ethylene dibromide tanks and four liquid chlorine tanks, all bound for Ellesmere Port.

From 1981 until 1984 Class 40 and Class 25 pairings appeared frequently on train 6E41, which carried liquid oxygen in cryogenic tank wagons from the British Oxygen Company plant at Ditton to Sheffield Broughton Lane. Nos 40141 and 25296 haul 6E41 past Grindleford on 5 July 1983.

An unusual Saturday evening freight working livens up Tyne Yard on 27 July 1985: Nos 37067 and 37046 pull away after a locomotive and crew change with the 6Z59 trainload of BOC liquid nitrogen tanks from Tees Yard to Polmadie.

Ellesmere Port site, which manufactured anti-knock compound for use as a petrol additive, and its bromine extraction plant at Amlwch. The traffic consisted mainly of liquid chlorine from Ellesmere Port to Amlwch and ethylene dibromide in the reverse direction, together with occasional tankloads of bromine from Amlwch to mainland Europe. Several different wagon types appeared on the Amlwch trains, including some diminutive 1950s stock, originally unbraked but latterly fitted with air pipes, which survived until the early 1980s. Associated Octel also dispatched anti-knock compound from Ellesmere Port to refineries in the UK and mainland Europe.

The British Oxygen Company (BOC) established a conspicuous rail freight operation to carry liquefied oxygen and nitrogen from its new Ditton works in the early 1970s. Trainload services ran from Ditton to Wembley, Wolverhampton and Sheffield Broughton Lane, and there was wagonload traffic to several British Steel plants and other industrial destinations. This traffic used a purpose-built fleet of highly specialised 102-tonne cryogenic tank wagons

with vacuum-insulated, stainless-steel tank vessels.

A relatively small, but fascinating, rail operation served Albright & Wilson's Marchon chemical works at Whitehaven. The works itself was connected to the BR network at Corkickle via a rope-worked incline, which, by the time it closed in October 1986, was the only system of its kind in the country. The main function of the Marchon works was to manufacture sodium tripolyphosphate, the principal component of powdered detergent. Regular railborne flows ran to West Thurrock, Warrington and Port Sunlight, initially using railway-owned CHO/CHP/CHV 'Covhop' and CQV 'Prestwin' wagons. The switch to using air-braked stock began in the early 1970s when a small fleet of bogie PBA tanks entered service, and the last vacuum-braked wagons were replaced by air-braked PCA tanks in the early 1980s. Other flows to and from the Marchon works were soda ash from Lostock and phosphoric acid to Ince & Elton and Barton-on-Humber.

BP Chemicals at Baglan Bay became a prominent location for rail freight in the 1970s following the awarding of what was then the biggest ever Section 8 Grant, worth £415,000, to set up a new flow of propylene to Shell Chemicals at Partington. This traffic used a fleet of TCB (later TCA) bogie tanks, painted in the standard livery for a pressurised load of white with an orange bodyside stripe. Baglan Bay generated various other rail freight flows: the inbound traffic included salt from Sandbach and acetic acid from Saltend, while outward flows included vinyl chloride monomer to Barry, isopropanol and ethanol to Saltend, and caustic soda to a wide range of destinations.

Another major Section 8 beneficiary was the Roche Products pharmaceuticals plant at Dalry, which expanded its rail facilities in the early 1980s to receive salt, sulphuric acid, caustic soda

The cable-worked incline known as Corkickle Brake was a fascinating operation that survived until October 1986, conveying wagons between the main line at Corkickle and the Albright & Wilson chemical works. Two soda ash tanks reach the bottom of the incline on 21 July 1979. *Tom Heavyside*

Class 25 No D7652 heads east near Grange-over-Sands with a mixed load of 'Prestwin' and 'Covhop' wagons from Corkickle on 21 June 1968. *Michael Mensing*

BR's fleet of covered hopper wagons, usually known as 'Covhops' and coded CHO/CHP/CHV for TOPS purposes, carried a wide range of powdered loads including soda ash, alumina, sand and sugar. A few brand-new air-braked wagons interrupt the string of 'Covhops' in this northbound train passing Drigg on 8 June 1976, powered by No 40095. *Gavin Morrison*

BR carried sodium tripolyphosphate from Corkickle to Port Sunlight, Warrington and West Thurrock using two-axle 'depressed centre' PCA tank wagons hired from Procor and Tiger Rail. Nine empty PCAs are included in the consist of Speedlink train 6P85, the 2215 from Willesden to Workington, as it passes Dalton Junction on 1 August 1985. The motive power is No 31293.

The Steetley chemical works at West Ham, located alongside the North Woolwich branch, received wagonloads of sulphuric acid from Avonmouth. No 31250 shunts TTA tanks at West Ham on 4 July 1989 after working the morning Speedlink trip from Temple Mills.

The ICI chemical plants at Stevenston and Ardeer produced regular railborne traffic in the 1980s. No 26038 shunts back into the Misk complex at Ardeer with four tanks containing caustic soda from Runcorn on 5 April 1989.

and even coal by rail. The operation at Dalry was geared to taking wagonload quantities and became wholly reliant on the Speedlink network.

●

As the 1980s progressed, so a large amount of chemicals traffic quietly disappeared from the railway. Changes in production and distribution patterns were often to blame, together with the ever keener competition from road transport and, in a few instances, pipelines. Environmental considerations sometimes worked against rail freight because full trainload operation tended to require the storage of large quantities of chemicals at the receiving terminal, which was considered hazardous. Fertiliser carryings declined in line with the fall in demand for synthetic fertilisers, with UKF (later Kemira) traffic particularly hard hit. However, Norsk Hydro, which took over the Fisons fertiliser plant at Immingham, bucked the trend by introducing block trains to Avonmouth and Leith in the late 1980s as well as Speedlink traffic to Alscott, Ashford, Holton Heath, Banbury and Aberdeen.

Stalybridge became a new destination for chemicals traffic when Atochem opened a siding in 1990 to receive trainloads of styrene monomer, used to produce polystyrene, from Immingham. Shell launched a flow of propylene from Humber oil refinery to Stanlow in the same year. Warwick Chemicals opened a terminal at Mostyn Dock, which began to receive acetic acid from Saltend in 1991. The European Vinyls Corporation gave

a new lease of life to the Fleetwood branch by introducing new wagons on its vinyl chloride monomer traffic from Burn Naze to Barry. But these new flows were outnumbered by traffic losses, which included some high-volume flows such as anhydrous ammonia from Teesside and the trainload liquid oxygen traffic from BOC Ditton. Many rail terminals such as Runcorn, Ellesmere Port and Haverton Hill saw their traffic plummet to worryingly low levels.

The demise of Speedlink in 1991 forced the axing of many small-scale or irregular flows of chemicals, but BR retained some former Speedlink traffic by switching it to block train operation, with a limited amount of tripping to and from individual terminals where practicable. Traffic from the BP Chemicals plant at Saltend was gathered into regular block trains to Mostyn (via Ellesmere Port), Baglan Bay, Spondon and Seal Sands. Chlorine traffic from Wilton to Langley Green had already been formed into a block train before the end of Speedlink, but from July 1991 this service carried other chemicals from Teesside to the West Midlands, such as carbon dioxide from Haverton Hill to Coleshill. BR also retained former Speedlink flows of carbon dioxide from Cameron Bridge and Mossend by running a twice-weekly service

After the closure of Ardwick West goods depot in 1990, Newton-le-Willows became the receiving terminal for carbon dioxide in North West England. Four carbon dioxide tanks for Newton-le-Willows are shunted by pilot locomotive No 08613 in Warrington Arpley yard on 27 June 1991.

from these locations to Warrington Arpley (for Newton-le-Willows) and Willesden. The carbon dioxide terminal at Willesden had opened as recently as 1990.

Warrington Arpley retained a limited amount of local trip working for chemicals traffic, with the carbon dioxide to Newton-le-Willows being conveyed by the same diagram that collected chemicals as required from Sandbach, Middlewich, Runcorn, St Helens and

Ellesmere Port. Most of the traffic from the last five locations was combined into a three-times-weekly service from Warrington to Carlisle (for Wigton) and Ayr (for Stevenston and Dalry). At Carlisle a further connection was made with a twice-weekly service from Port Clarence.

BR retained two former Speedlink flows on the Cumbrian Coast line by switching to Saturdays-only trainload operation, using traction resources that would otherwise have stood

Above The flow of sodium tripolyphosphate from Corkickle to West Thurrock outlived the demise of Speedlink and became a Saturdays-only block train. No 47205 passes South Kenton with 6A49, the 0910 from Corkickle to Willesden, on 27 July 1991. The wagons would travel forward to West Thurrock the following Monday morning.

Right Passing through the preservation site at Quainton Road on 9 July 1986 is No 31224 with 6B74, the 1225 Aylesbury to Wolverton trip working, conveying a mixed load including four empty fertiliser vans from Akeman Street to Ince & Elton.

Right **Liquefied petroleum gas (LPG) was a by-product from the Wytch Farm oilfield on the Dorset coast, which provided BR with regular trainload business for many years. No 60039** *Glastonbury Tor* **passes South Moreton with 6V13, the 1218 Furzebrook to Hallen Marsh LPG tank train, on 31 July 1991.**

Below **The steel industry was one of the main customers for railborne deliveries of liquid oxygen. Two BOC oxygen tanks for Sheerness Steel are marshalled at the head of 6O76, the 0855 from Willesden to Sheerness, as it passes Queenborough behind No 47326 on 2 August 1991.**

idle. One was sodium tripolyphosphate from Whitehaven to West Thurrock, which was the last rail flow from Albright & Wilson's Marchon works and had been loaded from road tankers at Corkickle since 1986. The other new train on the Cumbrian Coast conveyed caustic soda and other chemicals from Ellesmere Port to Plumpton Junction, and was later extended to Sellafield to deliver nitric acid from Ince & Elton.

The fertiliser plants at Immingham (Norsk Hydro) and Ince & Elton (Kemira) temporarily overcame the demise of Speedlink by running more trainload services. From Immingham new block trains ran to Carlisle and Aberdeen, using the same resources that already served Avonmouth and Leith. New destinations for block trains from Ince & Elton were Diss, Lugton and Thornton. The Diss train took the path of the now withdrawn train to Crawley, still detaching traffic for Akeman Street at Bletchley.

Traffic to Lugton and Thornton was conveyed by a new weekly service from Ince & Elton via Mossend.

The CIBA-Geigy chemicals plant at Duxford had been heavily reliant on Speedlink, and only two flows were retained after July 1991: urea from King's Lynn, which was conveyed by an RfD European service, and methanol from Purfleet, which was conveyed by a three-times-weekly block train. Another small-scale survivor of the demise of Speedlink was liquid oxygen from Ditton to Sheerness, which used a combination of Tiger Freightways and RfD services via Willesden yard.

In the run-up to railway privatisation, chemicals traffic continued its gradual decline. The 18-mile Amlwch branch lost its last source of revenue when the tank trains to and from Ellesmere Port ceased in 1993 in favour of road transport. The Partington branch closed in the same year after the loss of the propylene traffic from Baglan Bay. Further losses in 1993 were the Oakleigh (Winnington) to Larbert soda ash trains, marking the end of rail-borne chemicals traffic from the Brunner Mond (formerly ICI) complex in Northwich, and liquid chlorine trains to Langley Green, which had recently reverted to running from Ellesmere Port after a spell of operation from Wilton. The Albright & Wilson terminal at Langley Green remained active a little longer to receive imports of phosphorus. It was a similar story at Ince & Elton, where fertiliser traffic ceased in 1993 but the terminal remained in use to dispatch nitric acid to Sellafield.

All domestic chemicals traffic switched from Railfreight Distribution to Trainload Freight management at the same time as Trainload Freight was divided into the three pre-privatisation companies – Loadhaul, Mainline

The Albright & Wilson works at Langley Green, located on the stub of the former Oldbury branch, received trainloads of liquid chlorine from Wilton, as well as occasional wagonload deliveries of phosphorus from mainland Europe. Running as trip 6T48 from Bescot, No 47345 sets back into the sidings at Langley Green on 23 July 1991 before running round and propelling its load of chlorine tanks down the branch. The chlorine traffic ceased in 1993, and the phosphorus shortly afterwards.

Railfreight Distribution continued to carry chemicals on the Cumbrian Coast line after the end of Speedlink. Nos 31312 and 31229 pass Seascale on 2 July 1994 with train 6A49, the 0910 from Corkickle to Willesden, conveying four empty nitric acid tanks from Sellafield to Ince & Elton and 12 PCA tanks with sodium tripolyphosphate from Corkickle to West Thurrock.

Direct Rail Services ran a weekly trainload of nitric acid from Sandbach to Sellafield, routed via the freight-only Middlewich line. No 37609, one of the former European Passenger Services Class 37s intended for Channel Tunnel night trains, approaches Northwich South Junction with 6P21, the 1342 from Sandbach to Sellafield, on 31 March 1998.

Freight and Transrail – in April 1994. In practice, almost all remaining chemical flows passed to Transrail; the only exceptions were acetic acid from Saltend and styrene monomer from Immingham, which went to Loadhaul.

The various flows centred on Warrington provided ready-made business for Transrail's new Enterprise wagonload network. Transrail was able to withdraw some poorly loaded block chemicals trains such as Cameron Bridge to Willesden and reintroduce trip workings that fed into trunk wagonload trains on the West Coast Main Line.

Transrail introduced a new train plan for the Cumbrian Coast line, with the sodium tripolyphosphate traffic from Corkickle combined with nitric acid tanks from Sellafield. However, the sodium tripolyphosphate flow was lost to road transport in July 1994. The weekly chemicals train to Plumpton Junction for Glaxo disappeared from the train plan shortly afterwards. Another loss in North West England was liquid oxygen from Ditton, latterly destined only for Sheerness and Ipswich.

Chemicals traffic in the Ellesmere Port area continued to decline. Associated Octel still dispatched anti-knock compound from Ellesmere Port to mainland Europe after the main flows to Amlwch and Langley Green had ceased, but this traffic too ceased in 1995 because the Dover to Dunkerque train ferry was withdrawn and dangerous chemicals were not allowed through the Channel Tunnel. The last chemicals traffic handled by the Manchester Ship Canal Railway at Ellesmere Port was caustic soda from Eastham to Sellafield, which ceased in 1996. The remaining flow of nitric acid from Kemira at Ince & Elton to Sellafield became the first revenue-earning freight for fledgling operator Direct Rail Services in early 1996, but switched to running from Sandbach later in the same year, leaving the Kemira rail terminal disused.

While Direct Rail Services took charge of chemicals traffic to Sellafield, which included caustic soda as well as nitric acid, all other railborne chemicals flows came under the management of EWS after it had subsumed Loadhaul, Mainline Freight and Transrail in 1996, and Railfreight Distribution in the following year. EWS embraced and expanded the Enterprise wagonload network that Transrail had launched, and that was good news for several flows of chemicals, especially those to Dalry, which now included caustic soda from Seal Sands and acetone from Saltend as well as the established flows from North West England.

On the debit side, carbon dioxide traffic was phased out because it became more cost-effective to manufacture the product close to its point of use. The last carbon dioxide flow, which ran from Haverton Hill to Willesden, ceased in 1998.

RAILFREIGHT: CONTAINERS, CARS AND SPECIAL TRAFFICS

Above Carbon dioxide was carried from several distilleries and fertiliser plants to a number of railheads in the London, Birmingham and Manchester areas for the brewery and soft drinks industries. On 4 July 1989 Trainload Petroleum-liveried locomotive No 37893 leaves Temple Mills yard with the early morning Speedlink trip working to Bow, carrying eight TTA carbon dioxide tanks as well as Plasmor blocks in OCA and POA wagons.

Below Scottish Grain Distillers dispatched carbon dioxide by rail from its Cameron Bridge distillery on the freight-only Methil branch. Nos 20137 and 20148 approach Thornton with two tanks from Cameron Bridge on 28 August 1990.

Another loss was the vinyl chloride monomer from Burn Naze to Barry, which finished in 1999 when the source of supply was switched to a non-rail-connected site at Runcorn.

EWS trainload chemicals traffic, December 1999

Substance	From	To	Remarks
Styrene monomer	Immingham	Stalybridge	Also from Baglan Bay
Acetic acid	Saltend	Baglan Bay	
Acetic acid	Saltend	Mostyn	
Acetic acid	Saltend	Spondon	
Hydrocyanic acid	Seal Sands	Haverton Hill	
Propylene	Humber	Stanlow	
Propylene	Humber	Baglan Bay	

EWS wagonload and intermodal chemicals traffic, December 1999

Substance	From	To	Remarks
Salt	Middlewich	Dalry	
Sulphuric acid	St Helens	Dalry	
Sulphuric acid	Avonmouth	Dalry	
Caustic soda	Seal Sands	Dalry	
Caustic soda	Sandbach	Dalry	
Acetone	Saltend	Dalry	
Liquid dextrose	Lestrem (France)	Dalry	Intermodal; via Channel Tunnel
Terephthalic acid	Teesport	Workington	Intermodal

Meanwhile, EWS scored a major success in early 1998 when it won a contract with Eastman Chemicals to move 4,000 containers a year of imported pure terephthalic acid from Teesport to Workington, initially for a three-year period. This contract required the provision of 20 refurbished former Freightliner wagons and loading gauge enhancements on the Cumbrian Coast line to accommodate 8ft 6in containers.

Hydro Agri fertiliser: destinations served by rail from Immingham, 1998/99

Alscott
Avonmouth
Carlisle Harker
Carmarthen
Lugton
Falmouth (occasional)
Inverurie (occasional)
Perth (occasional)

A further intermodal development was the awarding of a £9.7 million Freight Facilities Grant to TDG Nexus in 1999 for a new terminal at Grangemouth, intended to handle chemicals from the nearby BP plant, which was being expanded.

Railborne fertiliser traffic made another temporary comeback in the late 1990s. Hydro Agri (formerly Norsk Hydro) reintroduced rail services from Immingham to destinations such as Avonmouth, Carmarthen and Carlisle. Kemira made a tentative return to rail in 1999 when it loaded fertiliser for Lugton at the AHC terminal at Widnes. Further Kemira traffic ran from Widnes and Warrington to Ely and Great Yarmouth. However, Kemira did not reopen its own rail connection at Ince & Elton and there

J. & H. Bunn fertiliser: destinations served by rail from Yarmouth, 1998/99

Bicester
Swindon
Andover
Gillingham (Dorset)
Yeovil Pen Mill
Wool
Chichester
Newhaven Marine
Hoo Junction
Sittingbourne

was little prospect of regular high-volume traffic because most of the company's regional distribution depots had been closed in favour of direct deliveries from the plant.

A new name in the railborne fertiliser business at that time was J. & H. Bunn at Great Yarmouth. EWS competed successfully for seasonal movements from Great Yarmouth to various railheads in southern England, using the Enterprise network as far as Wembley or Eastleigh, then dedicated feeder services as required. For a time these movements seemed to thrive and EWS even adapted a former Tiphook 'Piggyback' wagon to carry a forklift truck, which travelled with each train to facilitate unloading. However, the J. & H. Bunn traffic ceased in 2000.

Chemicals traffic in Cheshire received a boost in 2001 when Albion Chemicals (formerly BP) gained a five-year contract to supply hydrochloric acid to the DSM (formerly Roche Products) Vitamin C factory at Dalry. This traffic required the conversion of seven former petroleum tank wagons, which were lined with rubber and equipped with automatic valves. Meanwhile Ineos Chlor (formerly part of ICI) used a £4 million Freight Facilities Grant to part-fund a new caustic soda loading terminal on the Runcorn Folly Lane branch, with the promise of regular traffic in tank wagons to Dalry and in containers to Mossend. The first loaded train from the new terminal ran in March 2002.

Direct Rail Services continued to deliver chemicals from Sandbach and Runcorn to Sellafield, initially using its own resources throughout but later switching to a shared operation with EWS, in which wagons used EWS wagonload services as far as Carlisle, then Direct Rail Services haulage from Carlisle to Sellafield.

Cutbacks by BP brought the closure of all rail operations at Saltend and reductions at Baglan Bay in early 2002. Further losses followed. The rail system at Haverton Hill closed in 2002, as did the Hays sulphuric acid terminal at St Helens. The propylene flows from Humber refinery to Stanlow and Baglan Bay switched to Freightliner Heavy Haul operation in 2002, but ceased in 2003 and 2004 respectively. Traffic from Albion Chemicals declined, with the nitric acid to Sellafield being sourced from Teesside instead from late 2006. The last loaded hydrochloric acid train left Sandbach on 17 January 2007, by which time acid was no longer produced on site but brought in by road instead from Ineos Chlor at Runcorn.

In early 2010 the number of railborne chemicals flows other than those conveyed by general intermodal trains could be counted on the fingers of one hand: caustic soda from Runcorn to Dalry and Mossend, styrene monomer from Immingham to Stalybridge, and occasional wagonloads of nitric acid from Middlesbrough to Sellafield.

Ex-BR locomotive No 08523, owned by RT Rail, shunts six purged chemical tanks at Albion Chemicals, Sandbach, on 14 February 2007. This was the last operational day for Albion's rail terminal and the tanks were about to be sent to Shirebrook for storage.

5.

Nuclear

In 1968 the UK nuclear industry was developing fast. Several nuclear power stations had recently come on stream and the UK Atomic Energy Authority (later British Nuclear Fuels) reprocessing plant at Windscale, later renamed Sellafield, was the destination for their irradiated fuel rods. Rail was the natural transport mode for this traffic – which was often wrongly referred to as 'nuclear waste' – and suitable loading points were established as close as possible to each power station. The fuel rods were encased in flasks, which were carried to Windscale on a fleet of 24 purpose-built 'Flatrol' wagons dating back to the early 1960s. Windscale also received some flasks from mainland Europe via the Dover train ferry, as well as deliveries from mainland Europe and Japan via an import terminal at Barrow Docks.

As further nuclear power stations were opened in the 1970s and 1980s, so various changes took place in the use of rail transport. At Heysham and Hartlepool, direct rail access was provided into the power station, so that the flasks did not need to complete their journey by road. Between 1976 and 1989 BR introduced a new fleet of 52 air-braked flask wagons, coded FNA, which allowed the phasing out of older stock. In 1984 one FNA wagon was sacrificed in a 100mph crash staged by the Central Electricity Generating Board to prove the durability of nuclear flasks under extreme impact. The flask in that experiment suffered only superficial damage and its contents would not have released any radioactivity.

To carry imported flasks from Barrow to Sellafield, in 1977 BR introduced a fleet of six highly specialised well wagons. Coded PIA (later KXA) for TOPS purposes, they had four bogies apiece and a gross laden weight of 160 tonnes. They were supplemented in 1982 by three PIA

(later KYA) wagons with an even greater gross laden weight of 176 tonnes. BR also operated two KUA well wagons for occasional movements of nuclear material from Rosyth and Devonport for the Ministry of Defence.

No 40007 crosses the River Caldew on the Carlisle avoiding line with a nuclear flask train from Sellafield on 24 August 1981. The Carlisle avoiding line closed temporarily after a derailment in 1984, but never reopened.

Until the early 1980s BR carried nuclear flask wagons in normal wagonload freight trains and in some cases used public freight terminals as the transhipment point. However, the decline of the wagonload freight network and the need to avoid transporting flasks in the same train as other classes of dangerous goods led BR to set up a dedicated nuclear train network, with multi-portion trains splitting their loads at strategic yards such as Temple Mills (for Leiston and Southminster), Willesden (for Lydd), Gloucester (for Berkeley) and Llandudno Junction (for Valley and Trawsfynydd). Flasks were also conveyed to and from the UK Atomic Energy Authority research and development site at Winfrith.

Nuclear power stations using rail transport				
Power station	Railhead	Type*	Start of generation	Actual or expected decommissioning date
Torness	Torness	AGR	1988	2023
Hartlepool	Hartlepool	AGR	1983	2014
Sizewell A	Leiston	Magnox	1966	2006
Bradwell	Southminster	Magnox	1962	2002
Dungeness A	Lydd	Magnox	1965	2006
Dungeness B	Lydd	AGR	1983	2018
Hinkley Point A	Bridgwater	Magnox	1965	2000
Hinkley Point B	Bridgwater	AGR	1976	2016
Berkeley	Berkeley	Magnox	1962	1989
Oldbury	Berkeley	Magnox	1967	2008
Trawsfynydd	Trawsfynydd	Magnox	1965	1991
Wylfa	Valley	Magnox	1971	2010
Heysham 1	Heysham	AGR	1983	2014
Heysham 2	Heysham	AGR	1988	2023
Hunterston A	Hunterston	Magnox	1964	1989
Hunterston B	Hunterston	AGR	1976	2016
*AGR = advanced gas cooled reactor				

Flasks from mainland Europe routed via the Dunkerque to Dover train ferry were excluded from the flask train network and would continue to use general wagonload freight services in the UK until shortly before the closure of the train ferry in 1995. The traffic would then switch to maritime transport via Barrow Docks, as nuclear material was barred from the Channel Tunnel.

For low-level nuclear waste, such as used equipment, clothing and packaging that might contain low levels of radioactivity, in the 1980s BR introduced a short-distance service from Sellafield to the British Nuclear Fuels (BNFL) repository at Drigg. The waste was loaded in enclosed skips or containers and carried on two-axle or bogie flat wagons of various types.

When BR was divided into business sectors, nuclear traffic joined the portfolio of Trainload Coal, the logic being that both nuclear and coal industries served primarily the power generators. Nuclear traffic gained its own fleet of Class 31 locomotives, although other types were used in some areas, such as Classes 33 and 73 on the Southern Region feeder services to Lydd and Winfrith.

As privatisation dawned BNFL was one of only two companies – the other being National Power – to take up the Government's invitation to become open access operators. BNFL took this course for two reasons. First, the company was keen to demonstrate on

The 9-mile branch from Appledore to Lydd lost its passenger service in 1967 but survived into the 21st century to carry nuclear flasks from Dungeness power station. One of the Hastings 'slim-line' Class 33s, No 33206, is pictured entering the disused Lydd Town station with the inward flask train on 25 August 1983. At that time all flask trains required barrier wagons – former BR-owned ferry vans on this occasion – and a brake-van.

the international market that it could offer its customers a total transport package. BNFL already had its own ships, its own docks at Barrow and its own fleet of road vehicles. By acquiring its own trains the company would be able to take full control of all nuclear flask movements between various overseas ports and its Sellafield reprocessing plant. Second, BNFL was highly dependent on rail transport and was in effect a captive customer of BR. By running its own trains

Left **The railheads for most nuclear power stations were located some distance from the power station itself, requiring road transport for the last part of the journey. At the Trawsfynydd railhead on 17 April 1985, CEGB staff prepare to carry out the rail-to-road transfer.**

Below **Trawsfynydd power station looms large on the horizon as No 25058 passes Maentwrog station with the Trawsfynydd to Llandudno Junction flask train on the same day. This stretch of line had closed in 1961 but reopened in 1964 to serve Trawsfynydd power station, linked to the Conwy Valley line over a new connection at Blaenau Ffestiniog. Regular flask traffic from Trawsfynydd ceased in 1995 and the very last working took place in April 1997.**

Passing Stevenston No 1 box on 24 July 1985 is No 25201 with 7M22, the 1435 Fairlie Town to Carlisle nuclear flask train. The use of Fairlie Town as a transhipment point for Hunterston power station later ceased in favour of a new terminal at Hunterston port.

BNFL could potentially reduce costs, as well as having closer control of the day-to-day operation and security of its trains.

In July 1994 the open access ball began to roll in earnest as the BNFL board approved a detailed business plan, which led to the setting up of

Above **Temple Mills yard was the starting point for nuclear flask feeder services to Southminster and Leiston. No 37219 passes the then closed Temple Mills East signal box with the Southminster train on 9 July 1987.**

Left **Flasks from mainland Europe to Sellafield were conveyed by Railfreight Distribution wagonload trains until shortly before the Dover-Dunkerque train ferry was withdrawn. A flask accompanied by two barrier vans brings up the rear of train 6M79, the 1203 from Mossend to Bescot, as it passes Holme on 12 July 1993. The motive power is the unique thyristor control Class 87/1 No 87101 *Stephenson*.**

Left **No 25285 leaves the British Nuclear Fuels siding at Drigg with PFA wagons forming 6T60, the 1700 departure to Sellafield, on 31 July 1985. The outward service from Sellafield to Drigg carried skips loaded with low-level waste.**

Below **The UK Atomic Energy Authority research and development site at Winfrith received intermittent flask traffic for many years. No 33211 heads north through Eastleigh station with 7Z96, the 1100 Winfrith to Gloucester special, on 19 August 1987. On this occasion HEA coal hoppers were in use as barrier wagons.**

the subsidiary company Direct Rail Services (DRS). The new company had to acquire its own traction and opted for a small fleet of Class 20 locomotives, which it purchased from RFS in March 1995. Further hurdles that DRS had to overcome were the sorting out of third-party insurance and the securing of a workable track access agreement with the then infrastructure-owner Railtrack. These processes proved to be more difficult than DRS had anticipated.

By early 1996 DRS was able to run its own freight trains, starting with deliveries of chemicals from Ince & Elton and Ellesmere Port to Sellafield, and empty flask wagon movements between Barrow and Sellafield. In September of that year DRS extended its track

Left **Multiple haulage was a common feature of DRS-operated flask trains as they often conveyed two or more portions, each of which required its own traction after splitting. Nos 20304, 20305, 20306 and 20314 pass Brock with train 6K73 from Sellafield to Crewe on 28 May 2003.**

Below **Direct Rail Services kept members of Classes 20 and 37 going well beyond their life expectancy, and pairings of the two locomotive types were not uncommon. Nos 37688 and 20310 pass Hargrave with the 6K41 Valley to Crewe flask train on 23 October 2007. The flask wagons would complete their journey from Crewe to Sellafield early the following morning.**

access agreement to include loaded flask trains, and by early 1999 the only UK nuclear traffic not in DRS hands was the infrequent service from Rosyth and Devonport. DRS continued to haul its flasks using 'heritage traction', with further Class 20s joining the fleet as well as Class 37s. Trains were normally double-headed or 'topped and tailed', partly to insure against a single locomotive failure, which could leave a train stranded, and partly to provide greater operational flexibility, eg by avoiding the need for run-round movements.

The operation of nuclear flask trains had traditionally been made more difficult by the need to include barrier wagons and a brake-van in the consist, and by the imposition of a 45mph speed limit, which not only lengthened journey times but also made it harder to find suitable paths on the main line. The need for a brake-van was rescinded in 1997 and the use of barrier wagons was discontinued shortly afterwards. The speed limit for flask trains was raised to 60mph in 2002.

A number of flask train routes ceased to exist as the early power stations were decommissioned. Often the decommissioning period was lengthy: for example, the last flask movement on the Trawsfynydd branch took place in April 1997, some six years after the power station stopped generating electricity. However, in 2008 the Government announced its intention to build a new generation of nuclear power stations in the

Until the late 1990s barrier vehicles were obligatory, and a number of BR-owned ferry vans were redeployed in that role in the 1980s. Four such vehicles are included in the consist of 7V41, the 1722 Sellafield to Bridgwater nuclear flask train, as it passes Bootle behind No 25089 on 12 July 1983.

What is nuclear fuel reprocessing?

Reprocessing is a chemical process that separates the spent nuclear fuel rods into three parts. About 96% is unused uranium, which can be recycled. About 1% is plutonium, which can be made into mixed oxide fuel for use in reactors. The remaining 3% is highly radioactive waste, which is turned into a glass for long-term storage and eventual disposal.

The process at Sellafield begins with transferring the fuel elements – each of which consists of a uranium metal rod approximately 1 metre long and 3 centimetres in diameter – from the flasks into containers that are stored under water in cooling ponds to await reprocessing. Once the required degree of cooling has taken place, the magnesium alloy cladding around the elements is removed, a process referred to as 'decanning'. The fuel rods are then reloaded into insulated containers and are conveyed on internal railway wagons to the chemicals separation plant.

At this plant the fuel rods are continuously dissolved in nitric acid and the resulting solution is then mixed with a solvent known as TBPOK – tri-butyl phosphate in odourless kerosene. The solution and solvent separate out in a similar way to oil and water, and most of the waste products can be removed in the water-like layer. The remaining solution is then further refined in order to separate out plutonium and uranium.

coming decades. If those plans come to fruition, some currently disused track will probably be required again, at least for the delivery of building materials even if – as seems likely – the reprocessing of fuel rods is carried out on site instead of at Sellafield.

6.

Milk

From their earliest days the railways provided a fast and efficient means of transporting perishable goods such as milk. Initially the milk was carried in churns loaded into covered vans such as the Great Western 'Siphon G'. Some of these vans survived in regular use until the 1970s, although in later years they carried parcels and newspapers rather than milk.

The first purpose-built tank wagons for milk traffic appeared in the 1930s. All four pre-nationalisation companies acquired a fleet of them and BR commissioned further builds in the early 1950s. There were many detailed design variations, but most of the tanks were mounted on a six-wheeled underframe in order to improve stability, with an overall wheelbase of 13 feet. The tank barrels were always glass-lined and were often sloping in order to allow impurities to settle at one end of the tank. Rather oddly, the underframes of all milk wagons were railway-owned whereas the tank barrels were the property of the milk company.

The destination for most rail-borne milk traffic was the London area. The receiving terminals that survived in the 1960s included Wood Lane, Morden, Ealing, Cricklewood, Ilford and Vauxhall. The Vauxhall operation was unusual in that there was no siding and the tanks were simply parked on one of the through running lines and discharged by hoses underneath the platform. When empty, the tanks were tripped back to Clapham Junction via Waterloo. Milk loading points were once numerous and ranged from major depots acting as collecting points for a wide area to small wayside goods yards. Some flows were conveyed for at least part of their journey on the back of passenger trains, ensuring speedy delivery to the capital, although this practice ceased in later years.

Western Region milk trains, 1971			
6M16	1340	EWD	Whitland-Kensington
6M16	1600	SuO	Whitland-Kensington
6M12	1745	SuO	Whitland-Kensington
6M12	2025	SX	Whitland-Kensington
6M12	2000	SO	Whitland-Kensington
6C45	1555	EWD	Marshfield-Cardiff
6M11	1215	SuO	Penzance-Kensington
6M11	1450	EWD	St Erth-Kensington
6A17	1505	EWD	Penzance-London Paddington (also perishables)
6M19	1600	SuO	Penzance-Kensington
6B14	1610	SX	Ponsandane-Plymouth (also perishables)
6O19	1655	EWD	Chard Jn-Morden South
6M13	0155	MX	Southall-Kensington
6O02	0125	MO	Kensington-Morden South
6A02	0205	SuO	Kensington-Cricklewood
6A02	0230	MO	Kensington-Cricklewood
6A02	0325	MX	Kensington-Cricklewood
6O03	0250	EWD	Kensington-Stewarts Lane
6O03	0330	SuO	Kensington-Stewarts Lane
6E15	0236	SuO	Kensington-Channelsea
6E15	0244	EWD	Kensington-Channelsea
6V26	0400	EWD+SuO	Kensington-West Ealing
6O04	0640	EWD+SuO	Kensington-Stewarts Lane
6O05	1315	SX	Kensington-Stewarts Lane
6A03	1430	EWD	Kensington-Willesden Brent Sdgs
6A04	2205	SO	Kensington-Cricklewood

Much milk traffic was lost in the 1960s as customers turned increasingly to long-distance road haulage. By the mid-1970s BR's only milk customers were Express Dairy and Unigate, and rail traffic was limited to just a few key routes, mainly from South West England and West Wales to London. Among the more picturesque operations that survived into this era were flows from Torrington, Hemyock and Newcastle Emlyn, all located on freight-only branch lines. However, economic realities were soon to force the closure of such operations. The Unigate factory at Hemyock closed in October 1975 and the last milk train from Torrington ran in 1978, shortly before total closure of this section of the former Southern Railway 'withered arm'. The only milk traffic that remained on rail by the end of 1979 was one nightly train conveying portions from St Erth, Lostwithiel and Totnes to Kensington.

After the end of railborne milk traffic in 1980, the Milk Marketing Board made the surprising move of refurbishing 40 existing six-wheel milk tanks and building a further 31 'new' tanks on redundant four-wheeled underframes, the idea being to keep them as a strategic reserve in case of problems with road transport. For the first time the underframes as well as the tank barrels were owned by the private operator. The six-wheel tanks received TOPS code TMV while the four-wheel tanks were variously coded TRV, TRF, TSV and TTF. In the event, however, little further use was found for the refurbished wagons and they spent the remainder of their lives stored at various locations in South West England.

Milk made a high-profile but temporary comeback to the railway in the summer of 1997, when the then newly formed operator Direct Rail Services ran trials between Penrith and Cricklewood in conjunction with Harrogate-based logistics firm Tankfreight. The lack of suitable wagons and terminals meant that Tankfreight opted for an intermodal system, but

Still carrying its obsolete green livery, Class 35 'Hymek' No D7089 heads a down milk and parcels train at Pangbourne on 3 October 1968. *J. H. Cooper-Smith*

Class 43 'Warship' No D860 *Victorious* approaches Bath with empty milk tanks returning to the South West on 13 June 1969. The train had been diverted from its usual Berks & Hants route because of an accident at Somerton. *Hugh Ballantyne*

RAILFREIGHT: CONTAINERS, CARS AND SPECIAL TRAFFICS

Class 25 No 7575 passes Culmstock with milk tanks and vans from Hemyock on 14 September 1973. The branch had closed to passengers in 1963 but would remain open to serve Hemyock dairy until October 1975. *Brian Roberts*

Lostwithiel was one of the last surviving rail loading points for milk. No 47086 *Colossus* heads an up milk train past the Unigate creamery there on 15 June 1977. *Tom Heavyside*

End of the line for St Erth milk: redundant six-wheeled milk tanks form the main load for 7B43, the St Erth to Exeter Riverside wagonload train, on 11 June 1980, passing Liskeard behind No 50027 *Lion.*

Rail-served milk terminals, 1978	
Loading	
St Erth	Unigate
Lostwithiel	Unigate
Totnes	Unigate
Torrington	Unigate
Chard Junction	Unigate
Carmarthen	Milk Marketing Board
Marshfield	Cambrian Dairies
Discharge	
Wood Lane	Unigate
Vauxhall	Unigate
Ilford	Unigate
Morden South	Express Dairy

conventional ISO containers were too high to operate within many dairies and would have required lifting facilities at both ends of the route. In the event Tankfreight opted for bi-modal technology, using four of the ill-fated Charterail wagons and purpose-built tank trailers. The experiment was believed at the time to be a technical success, but it did not result in any regular traffic. A further one-off trial movement of milk took place in 1999, this time from Yeovil Pen Mill and hauled by EWS.

Direct Rail Services found further work for a few of the redundant Charterail bi-modal wagons when it ran its trial milk flow from Penrith to Cricklewood. Nos 20302 and 20301 pass Coppenhall with train 4Z58, the 1253 from Penrith to Cricklewood, on 4 July 1997.

7.

Parcels, mail and newspapers

In 1968 BR still operated a complex network of van trains carrying parcels, mail and newspapers. A number of cities had dedicated parcels stations, such as Birmingham Curzon Street, Bricklayers Arms (South London), Manchester Mayfield and Glasgow Salkeld Street. However, the bulk of the traffic was handled at normal passenger stations, many of which became a hive of activity in the late evening and early hours of the morning as passengers gave way to trolley-loads of packages large and small. Dozens of small stations, serving communities as diverse as Scunthorpe, Skegness and Slough, had one or more sidings where vans were left for unloading and loading during the day. At countless further locations staff would unload and load traffic while the train waited. The combination of detaching or attaching vans at some stations and making extended stops at others could make for slow progress: in Cornwall, for example, the first van train of the day took 3 hours to cover the 80 miles from Plymouth to Penzance.

The accompanying tables showing van trains scheduled to serve Newport and Crewe in the early 1970s give an idea of the amount of traffic carried. Those trains carrying mail and/or newspapers generally enjoyed Class 1, ie express passenger, status, whereas other van trains were scheduled to run Class 3, 4 or 6 according to their maximum speed, which in turn depended on the type of rolling-stock conveyed. Many normal passenger trains also carried parcels, mail and/or newspaper traffic; in a few districts, such as the Far North of Scotland, it was common for passenger trains to comprise a greater number of parcels vans than passenger coaches. Newspaper traffic was by its nature one-way and more time-sensitive than the general parcels business; newspapers tended therefore to be conveyed in dedicated trains, such as those listed in the accompanying table for Manchester. The empty newspaper vans would return to the appropriate carriage sidings – such as Red Bank for Manchester Victoria traffic – during the daytime.

Parcels trains at Newport, 1971			
2C70/4	F00	2315 SuO	Cardiff-Milford Haven (also passengers to Swansea)
4C03	2330	SuO	Bristol-Newport
3C07	2100	SX	London Paddington-Cardiff
4C00	0115	MX	Cardiff- Milford Haven
4M13	0020	MX+SuO	Bristol-Manchester (via Hereford)
6C26	2135	MX	Swindon-Cardiff
6C32	0035	MX	Bristol-Cardiff
4V03	2132	SX	Birmingham Curzon St-Bristol

4V12	1835	SX	Peterborough-Cardiff
1C33	0050	SX+SuO	London Paddington-Milford Haven (passengers and news)
4V09	2130	SX	Nottingham-Bristol
4V06	2110	SX	Oldham-Cardiff
1V56	0145	SX	Crewe-Cardiff (passengers and mail)
1V44	2055	SX	Bradford-Bristol
4C02	0435	SX	Gloucester-Cardiff
4C04/ 1C04	0630		Cardiff-Swansea (also passengers from Neath)
3V20	1830	SX	Sunderland-Bristol

4V07	0215	EWD	Crewe-Bristol
4C17	0840	EWD	Swindon-Cardiff
4C06	1235	EWD	Cardiff-Haverfordwest
4V20	1315	MX	Manchester-Cardiff
3V09	1918	SX	Manchester-Cardiff (also mail)
3V56	0002	SuO	Manchester-Cardiff
4V04	2346	SO	York-Bristol
3A45	2240	SX	Cardiff-London Paddington
6B04	2340	SX	Cardiff-Bristol
1M09	0002	EWD	Cardiff-Liverpool (also passengers to Crewe)
4E14	0145	MX	Cardiff-Peterborough
3B06	0457	EWD	Newport-Bristol
4B08	1930	SX	Newport-Bristol
4M08	1840	SX	Swansea-Bolton
3E08	2230	SX	Bristol-Bradford
4C24	2110	SX	Pontypridd-Cardiff
3E07	2250	SX	Bristol-Newcastle
1B30	2220	SX	Cardiff-Gloucester
4M11	2320	SX	Bristol-Nottingham

West Coast Main Line parcels 1971: trains calling at Crewe station

4F01	0008	EWD	Crewe-Liverpool
4H07	0042	EWD	Crewe-Manchester
4P06	2230	MX	Birmingham Curzon St-Preston
4H12	0120	MX	Crewe-Manchester Mayfield
1H02	2310	MX+SuO	London Euston-Manchester (news)
4M08	1845	SX	Swansea-Bolton
1F70	0154	MX	Crewe-Liverpool (news)
1P25	2250	SX	London Euston-Carlisle (postal)
1F53	0035	MX	Rugby-Liverpool
1F53	0217	SuO	Crewe-Liverpool (news)
1F53	0245	MO	Crewe-Liverpool (news)
1P45	0224	SuO	Crewe-Preston (news)
4H05	0236	EWD	Crewe-Manchester
4D11	0322	MX	Crewe South Yard-Chester
4M09	0002	EWD	Cardiff-Liverpool
4F12	0420	SuO	Crewe-Liverpool
4M13	0010	MX+SuO	Bristol-Manchester

4M20	1954	SX	London Liverpool St-Liverpool
4H08	0446	MO	Crewe-Manchester
6H05	0454	EWD	Crewe-Altrincham
4H06	0612	EWD	Crewe-Alderley Edge (EMU)
4M00	0032	MX	Gloucester Eastgate-Manchester Mayfield
4P15	0324	MX	London Euston-Carlisle
4M01	2238	SX	Southampton-Crewe South Yard
4H01	0916	MX	Rugby-Manchester Mayfield
4S17	1043	SO	Rugby-Glasgow Parcels Station
4S17	1050	MSX	Rugby-Glasgow Parcels Station
4K26	1332	MX	Shrewsbury-Crewe South Yard
4M22	1230	SX	Peterborough-Crewe
6K05	0800	SuO	Derby-Crewe South Yard
6D20	1615	EWD	Crewe-Chester
3P39	1520	EWD	London Euston-Heysham
6H12	1725	SuO	Crewe South Yard-Manchester Mayfield
6F08	1753	SX	Crewe-Northwich
4S14	1930	SX	Crewe South Yard-Glasgow Parcels Station
4P27	1930	SO	Crewe South Yard-Carlisle
4P08	1645	SuO	London Euston-Carlisle
6H12	2035	EWD	Crewe South Yard-Manchester Mayfield
4F06	2201	SO	Crewe South Yard-Liverpool
6P27	2209	FSX	Crewe South Yard-Preston
4K20	1908	SO	London Euston-Crewe South Yard
4F02	1925	SX	Nottingham-Liverpool
3S11	2045	SX	London Euston-Glasgow Parcels Station
1M58	1940	SuO	Peterborough-Crewe (postal)
1M58	2001	SX	Peterborough-Crewe (postal)
1S09	2030	SX+SuO	London Euston-Glasgow Central and Aberdeen (postal)
4M05	1250	SX	Penzance-Crewe South Yard
4J19	2106	SX	Shrewsbury-Oldham
4K27	2200	SuO	Shrewsbury-Crewe
4V06	2110	SX	Oldham-Cardiff
4V19	0015	MX	Crewe-Didcot
1M44	1905	SX+SuO	Glasgow Central-London Euston (postal)
1E73	0044	EWD	Crewe-Peterborough (postal)

RAILFREIGHT: CONTAINERS, CARS AND SPECIAL TRAFFICS

3M19	1910	SX	Glasgow Parcels Station-London Euston
3K04	0035	EWD	Manchester-Crewe
4V07	0215	MX	Crewe-Bristol
4O22	0240	MX	Crewe-Bricklayers Arms
6K23	0250	MO	Crewe-Stoke-on-Trent
1K93	0250	SuO	Manchester-Alsager (news)
4D02	0130	MX	Liverpool-Nottingham
6J02	0245	MX	Guide Bridge-Shrewsbury
3M22	2312	SX	Glasgow Parcels Station-London Euston
3A14	0845	MX	Heysham-London Euston
4A19	1135	MO	Chester-Camden
4V20	1315	MX	Manchester-Cardiff
4A19	1433	MX	Chester-Camden
3M14	1250	SX	Carstairs-Crewe
6G05	1725	SuO	Crewe-Birmingham Curzon St
4V01	1747	SuO	Crewe-Bristol
6P28	1753	SuO	Crewe-Derby
4K29	1909	SO	Crewe-Stoke-on-Trent
4K14	1841	SO	Manchester Mayfield-Crewe
3V09	1918	SX	Manchester-Cardiff
6K19	1927	SX	Northwich-Crewe
4K11	1930	SX	Wavertree-Crewe
4E22	2015	SX	Wavertree-Yarmouth
4K18	2032	SX	Manchester Mayfield-Crewe
3A65	1630	SX	Carlisle-London Euston
4O19	2023	SX	Bolton-Portsmouth
3A64	2144	SX	Liverpool-London Euston
4V05	2012	SX	Oldham-Bristol
4A10	1740	SuO	Heysham-London Euston
1K87	2225	SX	Manchester-Crewe (postal)
1K86	2235	SX	Liverpool-Crewe
3K10	2225	SuO	Liverpool-Crewe
6M11	2202	SO	Leeds City-Crewe

Manchester newspaper trains, 1973

1E02	0012	EWD	Manchester Victoria-Newcastle
1E04	0020	EWD	Manchester Victoria-York
1E66	0112	EWD	Manchester Piccadilly-Cleethorpes
1D00	0118	EWD	Manchester Victoria-Chester
1P55	0130	EWD	Manchester Victoria-Barrow-in-Furness
1E26	0215	EWD	Manchester Victoria-Leeds City
1P09	0305	EWD	Manchester Victoria-Blackpool North
1F65	0315	EWD	Manchester Victoria-Southport
1F54	0323	EWD	Manchester Victoria-Liverpool Lime St
1F13	0335	EWD	Manchester Victoria-St Helens Shaw St (DPU)
1J81	0335	EWD	Manchester Victoria-Bury (DPU)
1E49	2325	SO	Manchester Piccadilly-Durham
1E02	2335	SO	Manchester Victoria-Newcastle
1E04	0015	SuO	Manchester Victoria-York
1E26	0050	SuO	Manchester Victoria-Leeds City
1E31	0130	SuO	Manchester Victoria-Bradford Exchange
1P03	0205	SuO	Manchester Victoria-Barrow-in-Furness
1F52	0245	SuO	Manchester Victoria-Liverpool Lime St
1F54	0330	SuO	Manchester Victoria-Liverpool Lime St

In the late 1970s the Class 128 Gloucester parcels units were divided between Newton Heath, Chester and Reading depots. Newton Heath-allocated car No M55996 awaits its next duty at Manchester Piccadilly on 22 February 1977.

A selection of pre-nationalisation design parcels stock still in use in the 1970s:

Southern Railway-design Parcels & Miscellaneous Van (PMV) No S1468, shortly after repainting in Rail Blue livery, at Plymouth on 29 October 1976.

LNER-design six-wheeled brake (BZ) No E70696 at Bristol Temple Meads on 11 December 1976.

LMS-design bogie brake-van (B) No M31055 at Cardiff Central on 5 February 1977.

Van trains used a remarkably diverse fleet of rolling-stock, with many vehicles built to pre-nationalisation designs still in daily use throughout the 1970s. Even at the close of that decade BR retained more than 700 SR-design four-wheeled vans (PMV and CCT), more than 100 SR-design bogie vans (B and GUV), more than 300 LMS-design bogie vans (B), and 22 GWR-design bogie vans ('Siphon G'). Most of the 'Siphon G' vehicles were allocated to Western Region newspaper traffic, but the SR- and LMS-design vans could be found throughout the network; for example, an SR-design PMV was regularly included in a West Highland line passenger working in 1981. The BR standard-design van fleet consisted of more than 1,000 bogie gangwayed brake vehicles (BG), many of which ran in passenger train formations, as well as more than 500 bogie vans (GUV) and more than 800 four-wheeled vans (CCT). Some CCT vehicles were painted in 'Tartan Arrow' livery for use on the overnight express freight service between Kentish Town and Glasgow, which finished in the 1970s. The BR van fleet also included more than 70 four-wheeled former fish vans, re-coded SPV, which were to end their working lives on Post Office and Readers Digest traffic from Aylesbury.

In addition to using hauled stock, BR introduced a small fleet of self-powered diesel parcels cars for use on secondary lines. The fleet comprised ten Gloucester and three Cravens cars, later designated Class 128 and Class 129 respectively. They were allocated to the Western and London Midland Regions and worked mainly in the London, West Midlands, Welsh Borders and Manchester areas. On some routes passenger-carrying DMUs conveyed a parcels van as a tail load, a practice that declined in the 1970s and died out completely in the early 1980s. One of the last examples of tail traffic was actually fish rather than parcels: until 1981 an 'Insulfish' van with fish from Wick was regularly attached to a DMU from Inverness to Aberdeen.

Sorting mail on the move was a distinctive and long-standing feature of rail operations. The first Travelling Post Offices (TPO) dated right back to the mid-19th century. Not only did these trains allow mail to be sorted en route, but also

RAILFREIGHT: CONTAINERS, CARS AND SPECIAL TRAFFICS

Right **Electro-diesel No 73106 passes Grove Park heading for London with a typically mixed rake of parcels vans on 6 June 1979. The first three vehicles are a BR CCT, an SR-design PMV and a BR BG.**

Below: **Awaiting departure from London St Pancras on 20 February 1986 is No 45127 with the 2225 Travelling Post Office to Newcastle. This train had been transferred from the East Coast to the Midland main line in the previous autumn.**

some TPO carriages were equipped with nets for collecting mail bags from lineside posts without stopping. The last generation of TPO stock was introduced in the late 1950s, using the standard BR Mark I coaching stock design, and the fleet continued to expand in the 1970s as further stock was converted from passenger vehicles. However, the collection of mail on the move from lineside posts was discontinued in 1971.

Parcels, mail and newspaper traffic remained strong in the 1970s, but, as with freight in general, BR tried hard to make the operation

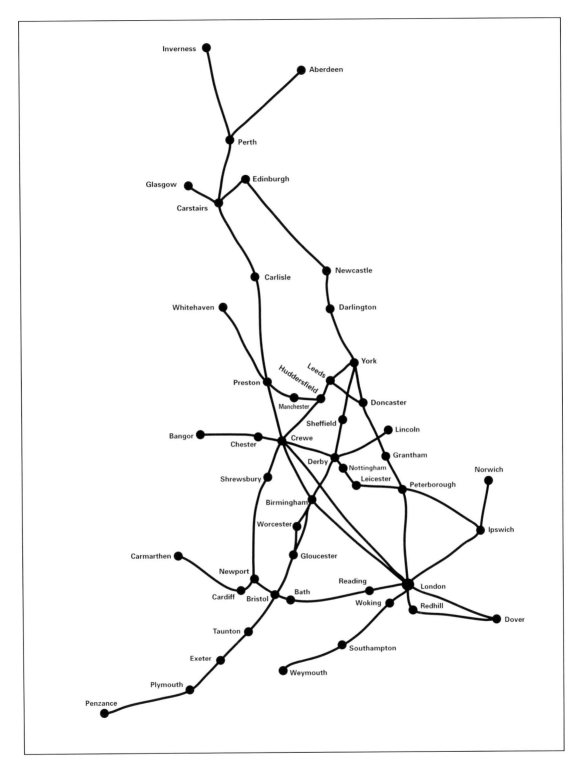

The Travelling Post Office network in 1971

more economic by making more efficient use of resources and concentrating on major flows. Between 1967 and 1977 the number of parcels carried by rail fell by 21% from 70 million to 55 million, while in the same period the parcels van fleet shrank by 34% from 7,401 to 4,838 vehicles.

During the 1980s BR scaled down its van train network as more and more customers switched to road transport. In 1981 the Rail Express Parcels service was discontinued; this led to the withdrawal of all BR standard SPV and CCT two-axle vans and of all pre-nationalisation stock except for a small number of 'Siphon G' and Southern Railway B vans, which remained

in use on London area newspaper traffic. In 1986 the Post Office ended its contract with BR to carry Royal Mail parcels, leaving just letter mail traffic on the railway. This move brought a further cull of BR's van fleet and the loss of a number of long-distance parcels trains, such as London Euston to Stranraer.

Another blow in 1986 was the decision by News International, the UK's largest publisher of newspapers with roughly a third of the market, to ditch its rail-based distribution system. This decision left BR's network of newspaper trains in a precarious state. Further withdrawals by newspaper publishers – notably the Mirror Group in 1987 and Express Newspapers in the following year – forced BR to abandon the network altogether, with the last dedicated newspaper trains running in September 1988.

The mail network continued to contract in the late 1980s. Among the

Super-power for a short parcels train heading east through Manchester Victoria on 25 July 1979: Nos 40035 and 40171 are in charge of a mixture of vehicles of SR, BR and LMS design.

On the Far North line, parcels vans were carried on both passenger and freight trains. Two BG vans are marshalled behind No 26032 as it pauses at Invergordon with the daily freight from Wick and Thurso on 20 March 1981.

PARCELS, MAIL AND NEWSPAPERS

Left The 21-mile Leamside line provided a useful alternative route for non-passenger traffic between Newcastle and Ferryhill until its closure in 1991. No 40141 passes the attractive North Eastern Railway box at Fence Houses with 5M48, the 1308 newspaper empties from Heaton to Red Bank, on 18 October 1981.

Right The Cumbrian Coast line retained its Travelling Post Office service until 1991. No 47525 crosses Eskmeals Viaduct with train 1E01 from Workington to Huddersfield on 13 July 1983.

Right No 31129 passes Hayes & Harlington with empty newspaper vans for London Paddington on 8 August 1983. The train consists of the usual mixture of BG and GUV vans, mostly in the all-over blue livery adopted for newspaper traffic.

Above **A few BRUTE trolleys are scattered on Platform 1 at London Paddington as No 47144 couples up to a short parcels train bound for Birmingham on 19 April 1984.**

Left **No 40009 passes Agecroft with 4J17, the 0630 Barrow-in-Furness to Red Bank parcels train, on 26 April 1984.**

casualties was the well-known Shrewsbury to York overnight train, which ran for the last time in May 1988. Many of the remaining trains ran with only a few vans and BR tried where possible to replace locomotive haulage with multiple unit operation. A number of redundant DMUs were converted to carry parcels, including members of Classes 101, 105 and 114. The conversion work included the fitting of roller shutter doors for ease of loading and unloading. Some electric stock was also converted for parcels use, and on the Southern Region the Class 419 Motor Luggage Vans could easily be redeployed on Royal Mail traffic. During 1988 Royal

PARCELS, MAIL AND NEWSPAPERS

The GPO unloading shed at Liverpool Alexandra Dock was already looking forlorn on 2 April 1986 when No 31434 was captured on film about to depart with trip working No 73 to Edge Hill Downhill Sidings. The site was to close just three months later.

Mail launched its striking red livery, which was applied to hauled stock as well as to diesel and electric units.

The year 1988 saw a major restructuring of the TPO network, which was the jewel in the crown of BR's then recently formed Parcels sector. The changes included a new overnight service between London Euston and Shrewsbury, a new service between Manchester and Dover bypassing London, the reintroduction of a northbound London King's Cross to Newcastle service, and faster services on the Great Western main line. There were also some withdrawals, such as

the loss of TPOs north of the Central Belt of Scotland, but some marginal services managed to keep going a little longer, such as those to Whitehaven and Lincoln.

In 1991 BR's remaining parcel and mail operations became Rail Express Systems, which also took responsibility for the Royal Train and some charter work. Rail Express Systems adopted

No 85012 departs from Northampton with 1A88, the 1000 mail train to London Euston, on 16 April 1986.

Bolton saw a big increase in parcels traffic in May 1990, with three new locomotive-hauled services that had previously started from Manchester Piccadilly. On 15 May No 47569 runs light into Bolton's parcels platform to collect 1C25, the 1625 to London St Pancras, while No 47616 awaits departure with 1V03, the 1423 to Bristol.

the red colour scheme that had been applied to parcels stock in the 1980s and enhanced it with a grey upper band and light blue and grey flashes – a scheme that was regarded as highly unconventional at the time. The traction allocated to Rail Express Systems consisted mainly of Class 47/4 diesels, together with a few Class 31s and a small pool of Class 86 and Class 90 electrics.

It seemed like the beginning of a new era for railborne mail and parcels traffic in December 1993 when Royal Mail signed a long-term deal with BR's Rail Express Systems division for a revised network of services to run from 1996 until 2006. By the time the network started, Rail Express Systems had entered the private sector, having been the first UK company to be bought by the international consortium led by Wisconsin Central Transportation, which would later be known as EWS.

The new Rail Express Systems network, known as Railnet, was based on a small number of purpose-built rail-served mail depots that would maximise the efficiency of rail transport and provide easy interchange between rail and road. The biggest depot was the Princess Royal Distribution Centre at Willesden, which became the hub for rail services between London and

Royal Mail unit No 325016 passes Winwick with the 1M90 mail train from Glasgow to Crewe on 10 April 1997.

other regions of the country as well as for road deliveries to London and much of the South East, including Heathrow Airport for international mail. The seven-platform depot could process 34 trains and 400 road vehicles per day. Other purpose-built Railnet hubs were established at Doncaster, Low Fell, Stafford, Warrington, Shieldmuir, Bristol Parkway and Tonbridge. Mail trains also continued to use passenger stations on some parts of the network such as South Wales and the South West.

An essential feature of Railnet was the building of 16 Class 325 electric units to replace hauled stock on key electrified routes. Built by ABB in Derby in 1995/96, the Class 325s had dual-voltage capability, so they could work on the DC third-rail route to Dover as well as on the West and East Coast Main Lines. They

Problems with the Class 325 fleet led to a regular requirement for locomotive haulage, mainly using Classes 86 and 87. First GBRf-liveried locomotive No 87022 passes Grendon with 1S96, the 1626 Willesden to Shieldmuir mail train, on 28 July 2006.

could also be hauled by diesel locomotives, giving them useful flexibility when diverted away from their booked route due to engineering work or a temporary line blockage. The Class 325s were owned by Royal Mail, in what looked like a conclusive vote of confidence in railborne mail traffic.

For TPO trains and for mail trains on non-electrified routes, hauled stock remained the norm. The GUV and BG vehicles were refurbished to allow the roll-on roll-off use of York containers instead of old-fashioned mail bags. The cost and inconvenience of run-round movements was avoided by the introduction of Propelling Control Vehicles, converted from

The Class 67 locomotives were built largely with Royal Mail traffic in mind, but their days on mail trains were destined to be cut short as Royal Mail pulled out of the contract it had signed with EWS. No 67011 passes South Moreton with the 1M06 Swansea to Willesden mail train on 27 July 2000.

Class 307 driving trailers, which were positioned at the opposite end of the train from the locomotive. As for the traction, EWS needed a replacement for its ageing Class 47 locomotives. The answer was the Class 67, essentially a high-performance version of the Class 66 that would soon become the standard traction for UK freight services. EWS duly ordered 30 Class 67s from General Motors, who sub-contracted their construction to Alstom in Valencia, Spain. The locomotives were delivered between late 1999 and April 2000, releasing the Class 47s for redeployment or withdrawal.

In 2002 Consignia – the short-lived trading name of Royal Mail at that time – announced that it was pulling out of sorting mail on the move, putting an end to the remaining TPO services that ran from Willesden to Dover, Low Fell, Plymouth, Carlisle, Swansea and Norwich and on cross-country routes from Penzance to Bristol, Bristol to Low Fell, and Cardiff to Shieldmuir. Worse news came in

Mail trains on the East Coast Main Line comprised a mixture of Class 325 units and hauled stock with Class 67 or Class 90 traction. No 90032 stands in Tyne Yard with a rake of Travelling Post Office and conventional mail vans on 16 July 2003. It will later form an evening departure from Low Fell.

June 2003, when Royal Mail announced that it was withdrawing completely from rail. Not only did this mean cutting short the ten-year multi-million-pound contract that Royal Mail had signed with EWS in 1996, but it also meant mothballing the Class 325 electric units after just seven years in service. The decision was largely determined by cost, even though EWS had reduced its price by 20%, and flew in the face of the Government's policy of reducing road freight.

During 2003 the network of TPO and other mail trains was gradually wound down. The last TPO train reached its destination on 20 January 2004, with just a few residual services for pre-sorted mail continuing into February. The Princess Royal Distribution Centre at Willesden was retained for road traffic, as were the Royal Mail terminals at Warrington and Shieldmuir, but other depots were abandoned, including

Bristol Parkway, which had opened just two years previously. The Class 325 units went into store, together with the large fleet of TPO and other hauled stock that had been used mainly on non-electrified routes.

While the prospects for future Royal Mail traffic looked bleak, EWS was developing a separate network of high-speed services for other parcel carriers. Following trials in 2000 between Wolverhampton and Law Junction with a Class 90 locomotive and seven 110mph vans, EWS built a dedicated parcels terminal at Walsall Tasker Street and by the end of 2001 it was operating a nightly train from Walsall to Aberdeen with a connecting service from Law Junction to Inverness. A three-year contract with logistics company DHL provided a reliable baseload for these trains. In 2003 EWS received a £650,000 grant from the Scottish Executive towards the £1 million cost of a new parcels terminal at Mossend, which would replace Law Junction, and the company later won an Award for Innovation at the International Freighting Weekly awards for its new lightweight and flexible design of parcel cage. Hopes of further growth in the premium parcels sector were raised when EWS purchased some former Mark III sleeping cars for possible conversion to parcels vans. Unfortunately, those hopes were dashed in February 2007 when DHL switched its business to road and EWS closed down its entire premium parcels operation as a result.

Meanwhile, a limited revival of Royal Mail traffic took place in December 2004, when GB Railfreight won a four-month trial contract to run two trains a night between Willesden, Warrington and Shieldmuir. This service brought a welcome return to service for some of the mothballed Royal Mail Class 325 units. The initial trial was a success and by late 2009 First GBRf (formerly GB Railfreight) had increased the service to six trains a day, all concentrated on the core West Coast route. Traction motor problems meant that the Class 325 units sometimes had to be locomotive-hauled, using various Class 86 and Class 87 locomotives. The trains between Willesden and Shieldmuir were

occasionally diverted via the East Coast Main Line, but without calling at any intermediate depots.

What looked like EWS's last involvement in Royal Mail trains was the running of a few pre-Christmas 'extras' between Willesden and Shieldmuir in 2007, using Class 90 traction and a mixture of GUV and BG stock. However, in 2009 came the news that DB Schenker (formerly EWS) was to take over the regular Class 325-based mail operation from First GBRf with effect from May 2010.

Although the regular mail train contract was firmly in the hands of First GBRf, the Royal Mail chartered a locomotive-hauled train from EWS for the pre-Christmas rush in 2007. No 90028 passes Winwick Junction with ten NBA and NKA vans on 17 December 2007 forming 1S30, the 1026 from Willesden to Shieldmuir.

Index